ANILHA
MW01618402

PACIFIC CROSSINGS

A PHILIPPINE COOKBOOK

PACIFIC CROSSINGS

A PHILIPPINE COOKBOOK

LILY GAMBOA O'BOYLE

Photographed by

BILL McCONNELL

ACACIA CORPORATION
NEW YORK

Food Styling: Roscoe Betsill
All food photos taken by Bill McConnell
Photos of chefs taken by Remy Bautista except Reynaldo Alejandro's and Regina Aguinaldo's which were taken by Lita Puyat
Photos on pages 6 through 9 taken by Jules Alexander, courtesy of Acacia Corporation
Editor: Kevin Clark
Production Coordinator: Bonjin Bolinao
Prop Styling: Lily Gamboa O'Boyle
Art Direction and Design: Chris Thompson
Spot Illustrations: Christy Hale

Library of Congress Cataloging-in-Publication Data
O'Boyle, Lily Gamboa
Pacific Crossings: A Philippine Cookbook/Lily Gamboa O'Boyle
ISBN 0-944863-25-6
1. Cookery, Philippine. I. Title.
TX724.5.P5025 1994
641.59599–dc20 93-12794 CIP

Printing supervision by Reyes Publishing, Inc.
Printed and bound in China
by Toppan Printing Co. (Shenzhen) Ltd.
10 9 8 7 6 5 4 3 2 1

This book is dedicated to my mother,
the most wonderfully creative cook I know
and to my father who instilled in me
the love of writing.

L. G. O'B.

In 1521, the Spanish set foot on Philippine soil. Before this discovery, the Philippine archipelago made up of some 7,187 islands was almost unknown to Europe. Only the countries of East Asia had a knowledge of these islands. The first Spanish settlement was established 22 years later after Ferdinand Magellan's landing by Miguel Lopez de Legaspi who sailed from Mexico.

The Spanish discovery marked the Philippines' formal introduction to Europe and established its place among its Asian neighbors. The conquering country, Spain, would bring the Philippines to Europe and the Americas through the Manila Galleon Trade. The riches of the East–gold, spices and silks from China would be loaded in the Philippines bound for Spain by way of Acapulco. The galleons would return from Seville bringing with them not only the European necessities for the colonists but the ideas and foods of a new culture.

The Dutch also made several forays into Philippine waters throughout the 17th century only to be repelled by the Spanish Armada. Britain occupied Manila briefly in 1762 and left behind Indian deserters who migrated up the Pasig River, made settlements along the way and intermarried with the Malays.

In 1898, the Philippines was ceded to the United States by Spain in the Treaty of Paris for $20 million dollars. This accord ushered in the Philippine-American

era which lasted from the end of the Spanish American War, through the Japanese occupation in World War II, until Philippine independence in 1946.

The relationship between the Philippines and its Asian counterparts harkens back to pre-colonial days. The Arabs were already settled in the islands in considerable numbers before the Spanish arrival. The Chinese, Japanese and Hindus also had permanent settlements. The Philippines was already engaged in a thriving cultural and commercial exchange with China, Indonesia, Thailand and Malaysia. In fact, what the colonists found was a culture whose family structure, diet, outlook and language was already formulated within the Asian context.

Needless to say, the centuries of transPacific commerce have not been lost on the Philippines and have had a tremendous effect on its dining culture. One need only observe the average fare of the Filipino family today to be struck by the effect of this blend of cultures. Aside from rice and fish which are considered staples, one may find noodles and eggrolls (Chinese), *adobo* (Mexican), *sinigang na hipon* (Malay), apple pie (American) and *halo halo* (Japanese). Regardless of their origins, these dishes have over the years been added to and transformed in so many ways there is no longer any doubt that they have become truly Philippine.

Raymond Sokolov, a writer on food and its history and preparation who travelled to the Philippines not so long ago, was right when he surmised after a lengthy analysis of the intricacies of Philippine food that, Filipinos "could embrace anything from abroad and make it their own" and that ultimately, sooner or later, "the whole of world cuisine can fit and end up Filipino."

Before I left the Philippines for the United States, 16 years ago, my association with Philippine food was mainly gustatory, an affinity I share with 64 million people in a place where eating happens to be the national pastime. Before the recent boom in Filipino restaurants, most Filipino food was eaten at home. Now, there are several thousand restaurants in Metro Manila alone.

Growing up in the Philippines I had the usual childhood experiences associated with food. I watched my mother, aunts and our cook prepare meals for birthdays, graduations, Christmas and the grand fiestas. Occasionally, I helped in the endless peeling and chopping associated with Philippine cuisine. I relished all the aromas emanating from the kitchen (one of the telltale signs of a Filipino household) and best of all, I ate.

When I finally moved to New York, I hungered for Philippine food. In the winter I would dream of fried rice and *adobo*—chunks of pork and chicken marinated and stewed in soy sauce, vinegar, peppercorns and lots of garlic. On blistery, cold days, I would pine for *tuyo*, dried fish fried and served with corned beef sauteed with tomatoes, garlic and onions—just like we had at home on stormy days during monsoon season. Summers, I would long for juicy melon grated in long stringy strands floating in ice cold water or *buko*, — fresh young coconut with its fleshy moist meat and cool delicious water, served from the shell and drunk with a straw. I was always on the lookout for green mangoes to eat with baby shrimp paste, *bagoong,* and plantains to fry with a little butter and sugar. Every once in a while I would have a craving so severe it would require an emergency trip to my mother's house or to one of the far flung Philippine restaurants of the city.

A few years ago, I went back to the Philippines after a long absence. Finally, I was back in food paradise! I sampled all my favorite foods from childhood, foods I had loved, known and remembered. I visited old haunts and celebrated with family and friends. Thus, the voyage of rediscovery began.

I was surprised at the level of sophistication Philippine food had achieved since I left. Of course there was comfort in the old tried and true standbys like *lechon, sinigang, pancit,* and many others, but the new dishes were a revelation. I ate suckling pig with *paella* stuffing, *sopas ariwanas,* a soup made of pureed squash from a very old recipe, jackfruit salad, blue marlin cooked to perfection in myriad ways, and *vichyssoise* of *ube,* made from purple yam, just recently becoming popular in the United States.

That homecoming visit inspired me to do this book. I was so impressed with the new group of chefs and what they were doing that I wanted to present them and their food to others.

I am pleased to introduce ten of the most creative and innovative chefs in the Philippines today. A number of them come from a long tradition of culinary families. Some are the progeny of well-known and established restaurateurs. There are those experimenting with new and exciting combinations of flavors, blending Oriental with Western cooking techniques, and those who are avidly resurrecting the wonderfully old-fashioned, regional cookery. All are well trained, highly individual professionals with their own distinctive styles, yet all, experienced in modern international cuisine, share great respect for the food itself, striving to enrich and enhance, never to mask the food's natural flavors.

I hope you enjoy these recipes incorporating the varied flavors and delicacy of the new Philippine cuisine, as much as I do.

TABLE OF CONTENTS

< Purple Yam Soup with Wontons (Ube Soup with Pancit Molo)

The Philippines is a republic of more than 60 million inhabitants. It boasts approximately seven thousand islands rich in wildlife, active volcanos, and waterfalls. The heart and heritage of this country is linked to a number of other cultures which have left their mark on its history. The contacts have largely been Western–400 years of Spanish rule, more than half a century of American administration, seasoned with the continual presence of Chinese, Malay, Polynesian, and Japanese influences.

The Philippines is primarily a rice and fish eating society. It seasons its food with a thin, dark and intensely salty sauce called *patis*, extracted from fermented fish, much like the Vietnamese *nouc nam* and the Thai *nam pla*. Coconut milk is used in many dishes, a distinctly Malay influence. The early Filipinos ate deer, pig, and a number of other game animals, fish and shellfish.

Unlike the other cuisines of Southeast Asia, Philippine cooking is not highly perfumed with herbs. Although Filipinos are accustomed to a wide contrast of distinct flavors, they prefer subtle flavor differences achieved through moderation and ingenuity.

The influence of China and Spain are evident in many dishes. There are a number of noodle dishes,

Philippine cooking is relatively simple. Although it may entail considerable chopping and dicing from time to time, most often it can be done with a minimum of fuss with no special utensils. Cooking is based on stewing, sauteeing, boiling and frying. Barbecuing, an American introduction, is also popular.

At a typical meal, all the food is placed on the table at one time and the diners help themselves. The dishes are selected at random. Rice is served with every meal. Like the Chinese, the Filipinos serve symbolic foods for fiestas, the New Year and special holidays.

pancit, which are of Chinese origin. The Philippine eggroll, *lumpia,* is also derived from Chinese cooking as are the dumplings, *siomai,* and meat buns, *siopao.*

The Spanish influence is easily detected from the large array of Philippine dishes that still bear Spanish names. The Spanish technique of sauteeing with onions in oil as well as the use of tomatoes and garlic have been widely adopted.

American food influences came in the form of pies and salads, hamburgers and Coca-Cola.

Some examples of these are the roast pig, *lechon*, stuffed chicken, *rellenong manok*, pork roll, *embutido*, baked ham, *hamon*, fried spring rolls, *lumpiang shanghai*, and noodles with sea food, *pancit malabon*.

PHILIPPINE MEALS

BREAKFAST

The Filipino breakfast, *Agahan*, is a substantial repast stemming from the Filipinos firm belief that it is good to start the day with a hearty meal. A typical breakfast includes a chocolate flavored porridge of sticky rice eaten with smoked dried fish, *champurado at tuyo*, or a meal of fried rice, eggs and *tapa*, marinated dried beef. Some people may prefer a Spanish omelet made of eggs, tomatoes, potatoes, and onions.

LUNCH

Lunch, *Tanghalian*, is another big meal. People who work usually go out to eat in a restaurant, cafeteria, or one of the fast food places. Traditional lunch fare is similar to dinner. At home, one may have soup, rice, an entree of meat or fish and a vegetable dish. For dessert, fruits or a custard with coconut or a jam of sweet purple yam can be consumed.

MERIENDA

At about 4 or 5 o'clock, people take a break for *Merienda*, the Philippine tea. One can enjoy crunchy cruellers,*churros*, dipped in hot, thick chocolate or sugared brioches, *ensaymadas*, with tea or coffee. There are many native cakes made from rice topped with fresh grated coconut and regular western type cakes and pies to choose from.

DINNER

Dinner, *Hapunan*, is usually the main family meal. Most people use western tables and chairs and eat with a fork and spoon. In some remote areas, people may still eat around a long low table and eat with their hands. A dinner meal can consist of spicy shrimp soup flavored with tamarind or *camias*, adobo, chunks of chicken and pork marinated in vinegar and soy sauce or *biftek*, slices of beef cooked in soy sauce and lemon and topped with sauteed onions. There can be *guinisang mongo*, mung beans cooked with bits of pork and shrimps and spinach. A mango salad made up of slivers of raw mango combined with tomatoes and anchovy paste can accompany the meal. For dessert one can have native fruit ice cream or *halo-halo* (canned native fruits and jams served with shaved ice and milk.)

BEVERAGES

Wine is not generally consumed with meals although it is gaining some popularity in the cities. More and more restaurants are now offering wine in their menus. Water and soda accompany most dishes. Some people take juices made from fresh fruit like mango, pineapple, and *guayabano*. *Buko* juice, the water from the coconut is a popular drink and is believed to be good for the kidneys. The national beer, San Miguel, is also drunk with appetizers called *sumsuman* and other meat dishes. Coffee and tea are served with desserts. Hot chocolate is usually drunk at breakfast and *meriendas*. There are two local wines, *lambanog* and *tuba*, made from distilled coconut juice.

The Philippines is witnessing the revival of a fine cooking tradition that goes back centuries. Moreover, Filipino restaurant goers in addition to participating in this revival are enjoying the birth of a new cuisine.

The new Philippine cuisine is essentially a return to traditional favorites and the refinement of the dishes of domestic cooks with the use of added imagination. It maintains the same flavors as found in classic Philippine cooking but is more lighthanded with oils. This modern cuisine is also easier to prepare than most of the usually labor intensive traditional recipes.

The adherents of this movement are mostly young chefs with impressive professional backgrounds. These talented chefs are taking homegrown ingredients and applying to them the techniques of contemporary Western cooking—grilling, smoking, blackening and serving on pastas and pizzas. They are not abandoning traditional Philippine ingredients or flavors, but simply combining these with what is available in the market, where the influences of climate, economics and history on cooking are brought to light. Like elsewhere, the chefs here are becoming celebrities, making media appearances and appearing in the annual "Chefs on Parade".

The recipes presented in this book reflect a cuisine that draws on the spices of the Orient and the fruits and vegetables of the Tropics. This new cuisine is easy to prepare at home. Like all the cuisines of warm climates you will find Philippine cooking to be a cool and vibrant cuisine, its foods refreshing and light, its flavors bright and clean.

REGINA AGUINALDO

Regina Aguinaldo graduated with a bachelor of science degree in home economics from the Philippine Women's University in Manila. She started cooking lessons at the early age of 8 and worked briefly for an uncle's bakery in her teens. Upon her graduation, she apprenticed and trained at the Hyatt Regency Hotel in Manila, the Max Chicken Restaurant and the La Taverna Italian Restaurant in Ermita, familiarizing herself in all aspects of the restaurant business from quality food preparation and menu planning to cost-accounting and inventory control. Since 1974 she has worked in the consumer services field of the food and beverage industry. In 1980 she started the Bon Appetit Specialty Food Shops, a chain of specialty foods and one-stop gourmet shops specializing in international foods and beverages, under the Rustan's Supermarket group. In 1989, she focused on the Bon Appetit Patisserie & Cafe. Working as Executive Chef and Marketing Consultant, she developed her own recipes based on home recipes handed down from her grandmother and parents, and applied the marketing skills acquired from her work experiences and travels.

The success of this expanding enterprise has been attributed to the popularity of Reggie's innovative recipes that are now marketed as the Reggie

Aguinaldo Signature Foods. She is presently based between the United States and Europe doing marketing consultancy, working on a cookbook series, attending food trade shows and seminars and studying food service operations and systems.

REYNALDO ALEJANDRO

Reynaldo Alejandro has cooked professionally in the United States, Spain, Brazil and the Philippines, and is a graduate of the New York Restaurant School. In 1982 he was restaurant consultant for the various restaurants of Bloomingdales for their Philippine promotion and was guest chef at the Le Train Bleu Restaurant. He was also the consultant for the first Filipino restaurant in Washington D.C., the Auberge Philippine à Georgetown.

He is the author of the *Philippine Cookbook, Flavors of Asia, Restaurant Design* and *Classic Menu Design.* He was also responsible for the recipe portion of *Philippine Hospitality*. He has just completed *The Pinoy Guide to the Big Apple* and is working on the *Philippine Christmas Book.*

Aside from conducting regular lectures on Philippine culinary arts throughout the United States, England, France and the Philippines, he also manages his own catering firm in New York City.

HENRY CANOY

Henry Canoy started cooking at the age of 15. He attended sales and service courses at the hotel and tourism school Ecole Les Roches in Switzerland. He continued his formal chef's training at the Swiss International Training Centre in Neuchatel focusing on service and kitchen technology and hotel operations. He later apprenticed at the Hotel Tete de Ren in Switzerland in the service and kitchen department. Upon his return to the Philippines, he trained with the late chef Antonio Perez of the Nielsen Tower Restaurant who taught him to rediscover the exquisiteness of Philippine cuisine, with the use of local ingredients. He later served as executive chef of Via Mare Restaurant.

At present, he is chef consultant of several restaurants: Cafe Isabel, Cafe Gianina, Gene's Bistro, The Smiling Chef, Viva Gelato Ice Cream and Pasta Bar, and Gino's Fine Dining where he is responsible for the overall quality and quantity of food production.

Together with Gene Gonzalez, Bambina Herbosa and three other young, innovative chefs he founded Alta Cocina Filipino, a movement devoted to the use and refinement of Filipino ingredients in haute cuisine, and the development of professionalism in the culinary field.

He is a regular participant in the annual Chefs on Parade sponsored by the Hotel and Restaurant Association and a member of the Confrerie de la Chaine des Rotisseurs, Baillage National des Philippines.

SANDY DAZA

Sandy Daza worked his way up the culinary ladder at L'Auxille Philippine, a Philippine restaurant owned by his family in Paris in the early 1970s. He started as a waiter and cashier and was thrust accidentally into the role of chef when the real chef failed to show up one day. Fortunately, Sandy had remembered most of the dishes from watching the chef at work on his free time. This experience sparked his interest in cooking. He later enrolled at the Le Cordon Bleu De Paris Cooking School and went to pursue a degree in hotel and restaurant management at Cornell University in Ithaca, New York.

After graduation he returned to Manila and managed his family's French restaurant. The restaurant closed shortly thereafter making him realize that he still had a lot to learn about the restaurant business. Humbled but undaunted, he continued to manage other restaurants creating and experimenting with new dishes along the way. Since then he has successfully managed a Thai and a French restaurant despite his limited grasp of both languages.

At present, he cohosts a television cooking show where he gets to create dishes for the different sponsors and hosts the cooking portion of a noontime variety show called EAT Bulaga where he gets to demonstrate the art of cooking.

GENE GONZALEZ

Gene Gonzalez is the young chef owner of the Smiling Chef, Gene's Bistro, Cafe Gianina, and most recently, Gino's and Cafe Isabel, two fine dining establishments created from a derelict colonial mansion.

Gene claims to have inherited his culinary skills from his Arnedo ancestors who were well known for their grand cuisine and elaborate entertaining. At the turn of the century, their ancestral home in Sulipan, Pampanga was the scene of lavish parties frequented by visiting dignitaries, governors-general, famous writers and royalty.

At 12, he was learning to cook under Nic Mazarraca, the well-known chef at the Italian Village Restaurant in Manila. As a young man, he went to France and apprenticed at Le Divellec in Paris and studied baking at the Henri Charette School.

He has been knighted by the Ordre Mondial des Gourmets Degustateurs and the Confrerie de la Chaine des Rotisseurs and promoted to Charge de Presse and Conseillier Culinaire, honors conferred by professionals in the industry.

Upon his return to the Philippines he opened a string of bistros and cafes. He is a founding member of Alta Cocina Filipino, the prime exponent of the New Philippine cuisine that endeavors to rediscover the romantic, nostalgic and modern possibilities of native ingredients in Philippine cooking.

Aside from being a chef and a restaurant consultant for food packaging and menu design, he is also a contributing food writer and was the Hotel and Restaurant Association Director in 1991.

BAMBINA HERBOSA

Bambina Herbosa studied cooking at the New York Restaurant School. Like some of the other chefs featured in this book, she learned the rudiments of cooking as a child from her grandmother and mother, who were renowned cooks from the province of Pampanga, long acknowledged as the culinary center of the Philippines.

After graduating from the New York Restaurant School, she apprenticed at several culinary establishments in New York. In the Philippines, she started a food and catering company called Old Fashioned Bibingka ATBP, named after a kind of rice cake that her family made famous. She is one of the founding members of Alta Cocina Filipino, and holds the distinction of being its only female founding member.

CELY KALAW

Cely Kalaw graduated with degrees in chemistry and agriculture from the University of the Philippines. But her love of cooking won out and she pursued the culinary field instead. As a child, she loved to play in the kitchen and watch her mother cook. Food and its preparation was a constant source of fascination. It was only fitting that when Cely opened her first restaurant in Manila she named it The Grove, *Luto ni Inay* (Mother's Cooking) as a tribute to her mother who loved to cook Filipino specialities in their kitchen. The instant success of this restaurant was attributed mainly to the attention to detail and innovativeness that Cely says she inherited from her mother. On any given day, one can find her in this wondefully ethnic restaurant that evokes the merry mood of a fiesta. Patrons are encouraged to sample a smorgasbord of Filipino delicacies spread out on three generous buffet tables. Cely believes the idea behind the buffet is the Filipinos love of fiestas and get-togethers. In this restaurant, one can try the best authentic local cuisine prepared daily from the freshest ingredients.

Aside from being the lively proprietor of this exotic restaurant, she is also a widely sought after lecturer on the native food restaurant and catering business. She conducts workshops and culinary reach out programs nationally, and gives cooking demonstrations on television and at various culinary schools.

DULCE MAGAT

Dulce Magat is the 26 year old executive chef at Via Mare, Manila's original seafood specialty restaurant. She holds a hotel and management degree from St. Scholastica College in Manila and a hotel and management degree from the Pacific Hotel Schools in Los Angeles. She also attended the Le Cordon Bleu de Paris and completed courses to earn the Grand Diplome de Cuisine, Cycle de Patisserie et Boulangerie.

After a brief kitchen and dining room apprenticeship at L'Auberge de Reillane in France, she was hired by chef Dante Lacarde to be his sous chef de cuisine at the Domaine of Killien Resort in Ontario, Canada in the summer of 1988. Upon returning to the Philippines, she apprenticed at the Manila Peninsula Hotel before obtaining her current position.

MILAGROS REYES

Milagros Reyes is a graduate of hotel and restaurant administration from the Ecole Hoteliere in Lausanne, Switzerland, and hotel administration from Cornell University in Ithaca, New York. She worked as executive housekeeper at the Hotel Royal Geneva and at the front office of the Hotel Beau Rivage in Geneva. In the United States, she apprenticed in the catering department of the Sheraton Inn in Knoxville, Tennessee.

At present, she is a consultant for numerous hotels and corporations and vice president and general manager of the Plaza, a family owned restaurant now converted into a food shop and catering center. Additionally, she is president of the Hotel and Restaurant Management Consultants Corporation.

NANCY REYES

Nancy Reyes' interest in cooking developed at the age of 10, when encouraged by her father, she baked her first cake. Later, she would follow this interest by pursuing a bachelors degree in hotel and restaurant management from the University of the Philippines and enrolling in summer cooking courses at Cornell University in the United States. At home in the Philippines she trained at the Manila Hilton and at the family owned Aristocrat Restaurant where she has over the years served as baking manager, catering director, business executive and a member of the board. Aside from being a talented cook she is also a food stylist and a columnist for several magazines and newspapers.

She has been a consistent member of the Chefs on Parade Committee. At present, she is director of La Truffe Divine Confections, a company that makes natural chocolate truffles.

APPETIZERS, RICE & NOODLES

The Philippine meal does not fall into the Western order of categorizing according to appetizer, main course, salad and dessert. Most meals are eaten family style with all the dishes laid on the table and eaten together. However, when using Philippine dishes in a Western context one may categorize them accordingly. Some dishes lend themselves for use as appetizers. The recipes that appear in this chapter would normally be side dishes in a Philippine meal used to complement the other main dishes.

Rice is the main staple of the Philippine diet. It is eaten with every meal. For breakfast it is usually served fried in oil and garlic and eaten with smoked fish or dried beef. As an alternative it can be served in a chocolate porridge or as a plain porridge with chunks of chicken, tripe and ginger. For lunch and dinner, rice is usually steamed or boiled and eaten with the main dishes.

Noodles are an integral part of the Philippine meal as well. There are numerous varieties and preparation varies from region to region. Commonly called *pancit,* noodle dishes are differentiated by the type of noodle used. Noodles also belong to the category of symbolic foods. Since they are believed to signify long life, they are a favorite for birthdays. Noodles can be easily combined with seafood, meat, poultry or any combination thereof.

< *Meatballs in Sticky Rice with Dipping Sauce*

FILIPINO SPRINGROLLS
(*Pinoy Springrolls*)

Yields 8

- **3 tablespoons corn oil**
- **1 tablespoon sesame oil**
- **3 tablespoons onion, chopped**
- **3 tablespoons raisins, chopped**
- **3 tablespoons celery, chopped**
- **1 1/2 tablespoons water chestnuts, chopped**
- **8 ounces white fish filet, cooked and flaked**
- **1/4 cup fresh green peas**
- **3 tablespoons carrots, julienne**
- **1 tablespoon sugar**
- **1 tablespoon white pepper**
- **8 springroll wrappers**
- **1 tablespoon flour**
- **2 tablespoons water**
- **2 cups vegetable oil for deep frying**

In a large skillet over medium heat, heat the corn and sesame oil and saute onions until transparent (about 2 minutes). Add raisins, celery, and water chestnuts; toss until ingredients are well mixed. Add the flaked white fish and saute 1 minute. Increase heat to high and stir in peas and carrots. Cover skillet and cook until carrots begin to wilt (about 1 minute). Remove cover and continue to cook on high until juices have evaporated, about 5 minutes. Stir in sugar and white pepper. Place mixture in colander to cool and drain. In a small bowl, mix flour and water until smooth. Arrange 8 springroll wrappers on a flat work surface. Divide drained fish mixture and spoon onto wrappers (about 1/4 cup per wrapper). Roll wrappers tightly and seal edges with flour paste made by combining the 1 tablespoon flour with the 2 tablespoons water. Refrigerate springrolls for 15 minutes. Heat enough vegetable oil in a large saucepan over moderate high heat until hot. Deep fry springrolls until golden brown. Serve with sweet pickle juice or soy sauce mixed with lemon juice as a dipping sauce.

- **1/2 cup butter, softened**
- **2 tablespoons garlic, minced**
- **1/4 teaspoon salt**
- **1 tablespoon minced, fresh parsley**
- **6 pan de sals (salty-sweet bread rolls), cut in half**

PAN DE SAL GARLIC TOASTIES

Serves 6

Preheat oven to 350° F.

In a medium bowl, whisk together butter, garlic, salt and parsley. Spread bread halves with garlic butter and place on sheet pan. (Cover and refrigerate any leftover butter for future use). Toast bread, butter side up, until golden brown, about 10 minutes. Serve immediately.

Chef's note: Pan de sal bread rolls are available in Filipino, Chinese or Asian food stores and grocers.

- **1/2 pound fresh anchovies or whitebait fish**
- **1 cup vinegar, divided into 1/2 cups**
- **1 cup water**
- **4 1/4 teaspoon salt**
- **1/4 teaspoon black pepper**
- **3 tablespoons fresh lemon juice**
- **1/4 teaspoon grated ginger**
- **1 small red chili, sliced**
- **3/4 cup onion, chopped**

PICKLED ANCHOVIES (*Kinilaw na Dilis*)

Serves 6

In a large bowl soak the anchovies or whitebait in 1/2 cup vinegar and 1 cup water for 5 minutes. Drain well and set fish aside. In same bowl, pour on remaining vinegar, salt, pepper, lemon juice, ginger, chili and onion. Let stand 15 minutes and serve on small appetizer dishes.

Pan de Sal Garlic Toasties

BAKED MUSSELS WITH PESTO AND MOZZARELLA CHEESE

Serves 6

1/4 cup coarse or Kosher salt
3 cups basil leaves, cleaned with stems removed
4 cloves garlic, coarsely chopped
1/2 cup olive oil
1/2 teaspoon salt
1/2 teaspoon pepper
1 cup walnuts, shelled and chopped
30 mussels (about 3 pounds)
1 1/2 cups (10 ounces) coarsely grated mozzarella cheese

Preheat oven to 350° F.

Pour enough coarse salt in a large sheet pan to cover bottom, (approximately 1/4 cup). To make pesto, blend basil and garlic in a food processor until finely chopped. While machine is running, pour oil through feed tube and continue to blend until a fine paste forms. Stir in salt, pepper and walnuts. Wash mussels, and place on prepared sheet pan. Spread pesto on top and sprinkle with grated mozzarella. Bake 13 to 15 minutes, until hot and cheese is melted.

MEATBALLS IN STICKY RICE WITH DIPPING SAUCE

Serves 4

1 cup sticky rice, uncooked
1 pound ground pork
3/4 cup diced fresh shitake mushrooms, stems removed
1/3 cup sliced scallions
1/4 cup water chestnuts, finely diced
2 tablespoons light soy sauce
4 cloves garlic, minced
1 tablespoon cornstarch
1/2 teaspoon ginger juice

Dipping Sauce:
3 tablespoons light soy sauce
1/4 teaspoon ginger juice
2 teaspoons chopped fresh cilantro
1 teaspoon sugar

Place sticky rice on a sheet of waxed paper. In a large bowl, combine pork, mushrooms, scallions, water chestnuts, soy sauce, garlic, cornstarch and ginger juice. Mix until well combined. Form pork mixture into small balls (approximately 3/4-inch in diameter), roll to coat in rice and place on a large sheet of wax paper (there should be approximately 26 balls). Place balls with space between each in large pot fitted with a steamer rack. If a steamer rack is not available, create one by placing wads of aluminum foil in the bottom of a soup pot, fill with 2 inches of water and rest an inverted plate on top so that the water level remains below plate). Steam meat balls in batches, for approximately 30-40 minutes per batch. Serve with dipping sauce, created by blending all sauce ingredients in a small bowl. Set aside until ready to serve.

CRISPY MUNG-BEAN NOODLES WITH CRAB
(*Malutong na Pancit Alimango*)

Serves 4

- 2 cups vegetable oil for deep frying
- 4 ounces cellophane (mung bean or mongo bean) noodles, divided into 2 portions
- 1 tablespoon sesame oil
- 1 cup fresh crab meat (8 ounces)
- 1/2 cup half'n half cream or heavy cream
- 4 eggs, lightly beaten
- salt to taste
- freshly ground pepper to taste
- 1/4 cup chopped scallions, for garnish

In a large pot, heat vegetable oil until barely smoking. Loosen noodle strands. Pull apart and unroll noodles carefully. Drop noodles in, a handful at a time. Make sure noodles are submerged in oil while cooking, they will balloon fully in 20 seconds. Drain on paper towels and arrange on a large platter. In a large skillet, over medium high heat, heat sesame oil; saute the crab meat, and then add cream. Season with salt and pepper to taste. Stir in egg and mix until runny (about 20 seconds). Pour over noodles. Garnish with chopped scallions

Crispy Mung-bean Noodles with Crab (Malutong na Pancit Alimango)

Bell Peppers Nancy

BELL PEPPERS NANCY

Serves 8

2 medium red bell peppers
2 medium yellow bell peppers
1 1/2 cups cheddar cheese, grated
3/4 cup bread crumbs, divided
1/2 cup light mayonnaise
1/2 cup unsalted butter, softened
1/2 cup coarsely chopped, shelled walnuts
3/4 cup raisins
6 cloves garlic, pressed
1 tablespoon Worcestershire sauce
1 tablespoon dijon mustard

Preheat oven to 425° F.

Lightly grease a large sheet pan. Wash and core peppers, cut lengthwise into quarters and remove seeds; set aside. In food processor, blend cheese, 1/2 cup breadcrumbs, mayonnaise, butter, walnuts, raisins, garlic, Worcestershire sauce and mustard, scraping sides of processor bowl, until well combined. Stuff pepper quarters with cheese mixture; approximately 2 tablespoons mixture in each. Sprinkle each quarter lightly with remaining 1/4 cup breadcrumbs. Bake 14 to 16 minutes , or until topping is golden brown. Serve immediately.

SESAME CHEESE STRAWS

Serves 6 to 8

1 egg
1 tablespoon whole milk
1/2 cup sesame seeds
1 package wonton wrappers
1 pound edam cheese cut into straws (approximately 2 inch X 1/2-inch pieces)
2 cups vegetable oil for deep frying

In a small mixing bowl, beat egg with milk. Place sesame seeds on a small plate. To assemble cheese straws, lay out 6 wonton wrappers and moisten edges with beaten egg. Dip 6 pieces cheese in egg mixture, roll in sesame seeds to coat and place 1 piece of cheese on edge of each wonton wrapper. Roll 1 turn, tuck ends in and roll up completely, egg roll fashion. Repeat with remaining cheese and wrappers. In a medium saucepan, heat oil to 350° F. To cook, deep-fry wonton wrapped cheese in batches of six, allowing for oil to reheat between batches for even frying until golden brown; drain on paper towels. Add more oil to pan if necessary. Best served warm. Yields approximately 40 cheese straws.

Chef's note: Another type of mild to sharp cheese may be substituted here, such as gouda, mimolette or havarti.

SEAFOOD COCKTAIL

Serves 6

8 ounces medium shrimp, shelled and deveined
1/2 pound squid, cleaned with ink sacs removed
20 mussels, scrubbed clean
1/2 pound cooked crabmeat
2 cups rice wine vinegar
1/2 teaspoon salt
1/4 teaspoon pepper
1/4 cup red and green bell pepper, chopped
1/2 medium red onion, sliced into thin rings

Over high heat, bring large soup pot filled with salted water to a boil. Blanch shrimp 1 minute, drain and set aside. Blanch squid 3 minutes, drain and set aside. Drain most of the water from soup pot, leaving 1/2 cup and fit with steamer basket. Add mussels, cover and cook over medium heat until mussels open, about 5 minutes. Drain mussels and remove meat from all but six mussel shells and reserve. In a large glass bowl, mix vinegar, salt and pepper. Add shrimp, squid, shelled mussels, crab meat,

chopped peppers and onion rings. Stir gently to combine. Top with reserved mussel shells and onion rings. Cover and refrigerate for at least 30 minutes before serving.

Serving suggestion: Arrange in an appetizer dish and garnish with fresh parsley or cilantro sprigs.

CRAB CAKES

Serves 4 to 6

2 tablespoons vegetable oil, enough for shallow frying
1 tablespoon garlic, chopped
2 tablespoons onion, chopped
1 pound cooked, fresh crab meat
1 cup cooked, diced (1/4-inch) potatoes
2 tablespoons frozen green peas, thawed
2 tablespoons yellow raisins
1 tablespoon red and green bell pepper, chopped
3/4 teaspoon salt, divided
1/2 teaspoon black pepper, divided
1/4 teaspoon + a pinch cayenne pepper
2 eggs
2 tablespoons whole milk
1 cup all-purpose flour

In a large skillet, over medium heat, heat vegetable oil and then saute garlic and onions until garlic begins to brown (about 3 minutes). Stir in crab meat and cook briefly (about 2 minutes) to heat through. Stir in diced potatoes, peas, raisins, peppers, 1/2 teaspoon salt, 1/4 teaspoon black pepper and 1/4 teaspoon cayenne pepper; set aside to cool. Next, in a small bowl, beat together eggs, milk, 1/4 teaspoon salt, 1/4 teaspoon black pepper and a pinch of cayenne pepper. Place flour on a large piece of wax paper. To make crab cakes, carefully shape 1/2 cup of crab mixture into cakes and dip first into egg mixture and then dredge in flour. Fry cakes in cast iron skillet over medium heat in 1/2-inch oil until golden brown; about 4 minutes. Serve immediately.

Chef's note: If crab cakes stick to your hands, wet hands in water before forming each cake.

1 pound *tagonton* (whole baby shrimps or shrimp fry)
1 egg
1 tablespoon + 1/4 teaspoon salt, divided
1/4 teaspoon pepper
3/4 cup cornstarch
2 cups vegetable oil for deep frying

Dipping Sauce:
1/3 cup rice wine vinegar
1/4 teaspoon salt
1/2 teaspoon minced garlic

FRIED BABY SHRIMP FRITTERS (*Tagonton Ukoy*)

Serves 4 to 6

Wash whole baby shrimps or shrimp fry thoroughly and drain well. In a medium–sized bowl, whisk egg, 1/4 teaspoon salt and 1/4 teaspoon pepper. In another small bowl, stir together the cornstarch and 1 tablespoon salt. Heat oil for frying in a small saucepan until hot. To fry, place a spoonful of the shrimp in the egg mixture and lift shrimp with a slotted spoon to remove excess egg, and coat thoroughly with cornstarch mixture. Place shrimp in strainer or colander and shake to remove excess cornstarch. Pat with a fork to flatten into a pattie and slide into the hot oil. Deep fry coated shrimp until golden brown and drain on paper towels. Repeat process for remaining shrimp. Serve with dipping sauce, made by placing all ingredients in a small bowl. Stir until well blended.

- 4 big leaves Swiss chard or Romaine lettuce, blanched, ribs removed
- 4 slices carp, fileted, approximately 6 to 8 ounces each
- 1/2 cup onion, chopped
- 2/3 cup tomatoes, chopped
- 1 tablespoon ginger, minced
- 1/2 teaspoon salt
- 1/2 teaspoon black pepper
- 1 cup coconut milk

ROLLED CARP POACHED IN COCONUT MILK *(Sinanglay)*

Serves 4

Spread the lettuce leaves on a platter. Place 1 filet on each leaf. Top with onions, tomatoes, ginger, salt and pepper. Wrap Swiss chard or lettuce leaf around fish and tomato mixture in roll-fashion. Arrange the rolls in a frying pan and add coconut milk. Simmer for 20 minutes. Serve hot.

Chef's note: Coconut milk, may be found in either canned or powdered (dry) forms in Filipino - Chinese stores, Asian and Hispanic food sections of specialty food stores and supermarkets. The carp, may be substituted with other white fleshed fish filets, such as flounder or sole.

- 1 1/2 cups white short or long grain rice
- 1/3 cup garlic, minced
- 1/4 cup olive oil
- 2 cups chicken stock
- 3/4 cup water
- 2 teaspoons coarse or Kosher salt
- 2 tablespoons fresh parsley sprigs, finely chopped

STEAMED GARLIC RICE

Serves 4

In large, heavy bottomed soup or rice pot, over medium heat, saute the rice and garlic in olive oil until garlic is tender (about 2-3 minutes). Add stock, water and salt. Bring to a boil, then reduce heat to low or simmer. Cook covered, until liquid is

absorbed and rice is just tender (about 15-20 minutes). Turn-off heat and allow to sit covered for 5 minutes before serving. Sprinkle the fresh parsley on top and serve hot.

Chef's note: If using an automatic rice cooker or cooking in a microwave oven, mix all the above ingredients, except for the parsely, in appropriate cooking bowl. Follow usual directions for cooking. In a microwave oven, the same cooking time of 15-20 minutes follows.

Steamed Garlic Rice

4 ounces bacon, sliced into 1/4-inch strips (1/2 cup)
2 tablespoons olive oil
1 tablespoon garlic, minced
3/4 cup onion, minced
1/2 cup pimientos, finely chopped
3/4 cup chicken stock
1 teaspoon oregano, dried
1 teaspoon black peppercorns, freshly crushed
coarse salt to taste (Kosher salt may be used)
1/4 cup parsley sprigs, finely chopped
1 16-oz. package cappellini or spaghettini noodles, boiled "al dente"

PASTA WITH PIMIENTO AND BACON SAUCE

Yield: 2 cups of sauce

In medium saucepan, brown bacon in oil over medium heat. Add the garlic and saute until light brown; add the onions and saute until tender. Stir in pimientos, stock, oregano, and black pepper. Season with salt to taste. Cook for 5 minutes to heat through. Stir in parsley and turn-off heat. Transfer sauce into gravy dish or mix with freshly boiled al dente noodles and serve with Parmesan cheese as desired.

Chef's note: To cook "al dente," boil noodles (other dried noodle shapes may also be substituted) in 2 quarts rapidly boiling water with 1 tablespoon coarse salt for 2 minutes. Drain and transfer to serving bowl. Dribble 1-2 tablespoons extra-virgin olive oil over the noodles and mix lightly.

SOUPS

Soup is quite an important feature in the Philippine menu. It is an ideal dish to start a meal although it does not always have to come at the beginning. Soups can be served with the main courses either on the side or modestly spooned over the rice, or alone enriched by additional ingredients. Such a soup, called *Pancit Mami,* is made of chicken broth, noodles, and bits of chicken meat, and is served with fried slices of garlic, hard boiled eggs, tofu and spring onions. There is a large variety of soups to choose from. Certain regions excel in particular soups. *Pancit Molo* is popular in the Visayas. It is made of broth with dumplings filled with ground meat, chicken and vegetables. There are also various *sinigangs*—soups made with either shrimp or pork combined with vegetables and enhanced with fruits that function as souring agents like tamarind and *camias.*

< Deluxe Mongo Soup

PURPLE YAM SOUP WITH WONTONS (*Ube Soup with Pancit Molo*)

Serves 10 to 12

1 pound *ube* (purple yam or blue potatoes can be substituted)
8 cups chicken stock or broth
2 bay leaves, dried
1/2 cup onion, chopped
3/4 cup leeks, chopped
1/4 teaspoon salt
1/8 teaspoon ground white pepper
6 pieces *pandan* (screwpine) leaves
1 pinch thyme, dried
3/4 cup heavy cream
1/2 cup butter
wontons (see wonton recipe)
5-6 pieces fresh coconut shells, halved with flesh and coconut juice discarded
1/2 cup chopped parsley, for garnish

Wonton (*Pancit Molo*)

1 1/2 tablespoons butter
1 tablespoon onion, finely chopped
1/2 tablespoon celery leaves, finely chopped
1/4 pound ham, coarsely chopped
salt and pepper to taste
1 tablespoon heavy cream
50-60 pieces wonton (molo) wrapper
1/4 cup cornstarch
1/4 cup cold water

Peel the *ube* (purple yam or blue potatoes) and wash thoroughly. Slice into bite-size pieces. Put into a saucepan, add stock, bay leaves, onion, leeks, salt, pepper . Bring to a boil until the yams or potatoes are cooked tender. Lift out the yams; remove the bay leaves from the stock. Set aside the stock. Blenderize the yams. Strain the stock and return to saucepan. Pour the yams into stock and bring to a boil with the *pandan* leaves. Continue to cook to reduce liquid until a slightly thicker texture is reached. Add thyme and seasoning to adjust taste. Stir in the heavy cream until well blended; add the butter to create a shine in the soup. Add the wontons (*pancit molo*). Cook for about 10 minutes or until tender. Remove saucepan from heat. Prepare the coconut shells as soup bowls. Pour in the hot soup and arrange the wontons, about 4-6 pieces per bowl. Garnish with chopped parsley and serve at once.

Wontons (*Pancit Molo*):

To prepare molo or wonton filling, saute the vegetables in butter until tender. Add the ham and seasonings, then the heavy cream. Prepare the wrappers by separating them one-by-one. Make a paste by combining the cornstarch and cold water. To wrap

wontons (*pancit molo*), take a wrapper and place approximately a half teaspoon of filling in center of wrapper. Fold diagonally, envelope fashion, and seal edges with cornstarch paste. Repeat until all wrappers are used up.

Chef's note: Pandan leaves (screwpine)- may be found in Asian markets. This soup can be served cold without the wontons like a Vichyssoise.

STUFFED YELLOW SQUASH BLOSSOM SOUP

Serves 4

2 tablespoons butter
1 cup chopped onion, divided
2 1/2 cups chicken broth
2 1/2 cups cooked, pureed, yellow squash (*kalabasa*) or pumpkin (winter squash may be susbtituted)

Squash Blossoms:

1/3 cup fresh mushrooms, finely chopped
1 tablespoon reserved sauteed onion
1 teaspoon fresh coriander or cilantro, chopped
salt to taste
freshly ground black pepper
4 fresh squash blossoms
4 slices of French baguette
unsalted butter

In a large soup pot, heat 2 tablespoons butter over medium heat. Saute onions for 10 minutes. Reserve 1 tablespoon onion for squash blossoms. Combine broth and yellow squash (*kalabasa*) or pumpkin and stir into onion mixture. Simmer 10 minutes. Meanwhile, prepare the squash blossoms: mix mushrooms, reserved onion, coriander or cilantro, salt and pepper and stuff in each of the 4 blossoms. Steam for 6 to 8 minutes until filling is hot. Rub slices of French baguette with unsalted butter. Toast or pan fry until golden brown. Divide soup into 4 bowls. Float a crouton on top (made from the French baguette). Top each crouton with a steamed blossom. Serve hot.

CONSOMME OF LAMB

Serves 6 to 8

2 1/2 pounds lamb shoulder, cut into pieces
2 carrots, cubed
1 1/4 cups leeks, cubed
1 cup onion, chopped
1 sprig each fresh mint and rosemary
6 basil leaves
2 cloves garlic, crushed
1 teaspoon black peppercorns
1/2 teaspoon salt
1 1/2 cups white wine
1 quart water or lamb or game stock
6-8 pieces of feta or mozzarella cheese, sliced about 1/8-inch thick

Preheat oven to 350° F.

In a large roasting pan, mix lamb, carrots, leeks, onion, herbs, garlic, peppercorns and salt. Roast for approximately 45 minutes, until meat is browned, turning several times. Remove roasting pan from oven and transfer browned meat and vegetables to a large soup pot. Pour off fat from roasting pan; deglaze with wine and stir with wooden spoon to dissolve any browned material in bottom of pan; add to soup pot. Add lamb or game stock or water to soup pot, enough to cover meat and bring to a boil. Simmer 1 1/2 hours, skimming off fat and scum until liquid is rich tasting. Strain broth through a fine sieve, lined with cheesecloth, and clarify if desired. Serve consomme in demi-tasse or consomme cups and garnish top with round slices of feta or mozzarella cheese.

Chef's note: You can use the meat as a stew adding in tomato sauce, pepper, potato and chilies to create a "kaldereta," (spicy lamb stew). Deglaze—means to reduce pan juices into a concentrated mixture with wine.

4 cups clam juice or fish stock
2 cups water
1 cup heavy cream
5 sprigs dill
6 ounces smoked salmon or mackerel, sliced julienne style and divided
1 cup creme fraiche
2 teaspoons sugar
salt and pepper to taste
dill sprigs, to garnish

SMOKED MACKEREL *(Tanguingue)* BISQUE

Serves 6 to 8

In a medium soup pot, stir together clam juice or fish stock, water, cream and dill. Bring to a boil, reduce heat and simmer, uncovered, for 15 minutes, until slightly thickened. Add 1 cup of the julienned salmon or mackerel, and simmer 10 minutes. Strain the soup, return to pot and stir in 1 cup creme fraiche and 2 teaspoons sugar; simmer 15-20 minutes until soup is thickened. Season with salt and pepper to taste. To serve, ladle soup into soup bowls and garnish with remaining julienned salmon and dill sprigs.

Chef's note: Other smoked fish, like herring and kipper, may be substituted for the salmon or mackerel. Creme fraiche can be bought from grocery stores and gourmet food shops. You can make it yourself by stirring 2 tablespoons of buttermilk into one cup of heavy cream. Allow to sit at room temperature untill the mixture thickens, usually overnight. Cover and refrigerate. This will yeild one cup.

6 cups chicken broth
Cheesecloth herbal sachet containing fresh mint leaves, basil, rosemary, thyme, parsley, cilantro, bay leaf and black peppercorns
2 tablespoons tapioca
salt and pepper to taste
1/4 cup chopped parsley

HERBAL FUMET WITH TAPIOCA

Serves 4 to 6

In a large saucepan, over high heat, bring chicken broth to a simmer. Add herbal sachet, cover and simmer for 30 minutes. Remove sachet and sprinkle simmering broth with tapioca, stirring well to prevent lumping. Simmer, covered, for another 6 to 8 minutes until tapioca is cooked through. Remove from heat and let stand 10 minutes. To serve, reheat if necessary; season with salt and pepper to taste. Stir in chopped parsley.

Chef's Note: Tapioca is available in different sizes. Cooking time may differ with the size of the tapioca. Consult package instructions for appropriate cooking requirements.

SHRIMP BISQUE (*Sinigang na Hipon*)

Serves 6 to 8

8 cups rice washing *(see Chef's note)*
3/4 cup white radish, peeled and sliced
4 ounces string beans, cut into 2-inch lengths
1 medium onion, chopped
2 jalapeno peppers, seeded and chopped
1 pound large shrimp, shelled and deveined
1/4 cup fresh lemon juice
2 cups watercress, trimmed and cut into 2-inch lengths
2 tablespoons fish sauce (*patis*) to taste

In a large soup pot, bring rice washing to a boil. Reduce heat to simmer, add radish, string beans, onions and peppers and cook for 8 minutes. Add shrimp and lemon juice and continue to simmer. When prawns turn reddish, add watercress and season with fish sauce. Continue to simmer for 2 minutes. Serve immediately.

Chef's note: Rice washing is water derived from washing rice the first time.

NATIVE MUSHROOM SOUP WITH PEPPER LEAVES

Serves 4 to 6

2 tablespoons vegetable oil
6 cloves garlic, crushed
1/2 pound oyster mushrooms, sliced
1/2 pound shitake mushrooms, stems removed and sliced
4 cups chicken broth
fish sauce (*patis*), to taste
ground black pepper, to taste
12 whole pepper leaves or other bitter green leaves, to taste

Heat oil in a soup pot. Saute garlic until light brown, 3-5 minutes. Stir in mushrooms. Cook for 3 minutes, stirring occasionally. Add broth, heat to boil, cover and simmer for 5 minutes. Season with fish sauce (*patis*) and black pepper. Add pepper leaves. Serve immediately.

SHRIMP AND CUCUMBER SOUP

Serves 4 to 6

- 1 1/2 tablespoons garlic, minced
- 1 medium onion, finely chopped
- 1/4 cup sesame oil
- 10-12 jumbo shrimp, peeled, deveined and sliced diagonally into 1/4-inch pieces
- 1/2 large cucumber, sliced lengthwise, seeded and sliced julienne style (about 1 cup)
- 3 cups water
- 1/8 teaspoon pepper
- coarse or Kosher salt to taste

In a soup pot, over medium heat, saute garlic and onions in oil until tender (about 4 minutes). Add the shrimp and cucumber and stir fry for 1 minute. Pour in water and add pepper; bring to a boil. Add salt to taste. Turn off heat and serve immediately.

SWEET CORN SOUP WITH HERBS

Serves 4 to 6

- 1 tablespoon garlic, minced
- 1/2 cup onion, chopped
- 1 tablespoon corn oil
- 4 1/2 cups chicken stock
- 2 teaspoons coarse or Kosher salt
- 1/8 teaspoon black pepper
- 1 can (8 ounces) cream of corn
- 1 tablespoon scallion, finely chopped
- 1/4 cup coriander or cilantro leaves

In a medium soup pot, over medium heat, saute the garlic and onions in the oil until tender, about 3 minutes. Add in the chicken stock, salt and pepper; cover pot and bring to a quick boil. Remove cover, stir in the cream of corn and cook until heated through. Check seasoning and stir in scallion and coriander or cilantro leaves. Serve immediately.

DELUXE MONGO SOUP

Serves 8 to 10

4 ounces bacon, cut into 1/4-inch strips
1 cup onion, chopped
1 tablespoon garlic, minced
1 medium tomato, cored and chopped
1 16-ounce package dry mongo beans, soaked in warm water overnight, drained
6 salted dried shrimp (*hibe*), soaked in warm water 15 minutes, diced
4 cups water
1 tablespoon coarse or Kosher salt
1 teaspoon black peppercorns, coarsely ground
1/4 cup red wine
1 teaspoon paprika
1 tablespoon fish sauce (*patis*)
2 tablespoons olive oil
1 cup fresh pepper or spinach leaves

In a large soup pot, over medium heat, saute bacon until golden brown and fat is rendered. Add the onions and garlic and saute until tender (about 4 minutes). Stir in tomatoes and continue cooking 3 minutes. Stir in mongo beans, dried shrimp, water, salt and pepper. Bring to boil over high heat. Reduce heat to low and simmer, covered, for 25-30 minutes or until beans are tender. Stir in the red wine and paprika; cook, uncovered, for another 5 minutes. Stir in patis and continue to cook for 1 minute. Remove from heat and adjust seasonings to taste. Stir in the olive oil and cook through for 1 minute. Turn-off heat and stir in fresh pepper or spinach leaves and let sit for 1 minute. Serve immediately.

Chef's note: Patis, is a fermented sauce derived from dried salted fish. It's found bottled in Asian specialty stores and food sections of supermarkets and grocers.

SALADS

The Americans are credited with introducing salad into the Philippine menu. Salads have become quite popular – especially with the diet conscious. Philippine salads consist mostly of native greens, fruits and pickled vegetables. They are mostly served to accompany and enhance main dishes. Among the common greens available are mustard greens (*mustasa*), Chinese cabbage (*petsay tsina*), amaranth (*kulitis*), swamp cabbage (*kangkong*) and ferns (*pako*). There are also the young tendrils of the sweet potato (*camote*) chayote, bitter squash (*ampalaya*), pumpkin and mango. Wild greens like parrot leaf (*kutsarita*), spinach (*espinaka*) and purslane (*olasiman*) can also be found. Blanched, boiled or pickled, the vegetables and greens can be served with a dressing made of *bagoong,* a salty shrimp or anchovy paste or one made of finely diced tomatoes, ginger, onions, salted eggs and hot pepper.

< *Zarzuela Salad*

1 pound hearts of palm, fresh or, frozen and thawed
4 salted red eggs
1/2 cup red wine vinegar
2 teaspoons dry mustard
1 1/4 cups light olive oil
salt and pepper to taste
2 egg yolks
4 lettuce leaves formed into cups
2 egg whites, hard boiled and sliced julienne style
salad greens to garnish (watercress, scallions, pepper sprouts or as available in season)

ZARZUELA SALAD

Serves 4

Slice hearts of palm julienne style into strips and blanch. Transfer to bowl of ice water and set aside. Cut salted eggs and separate the yolks from the whites. Slice egg whites julienne style strips; set aside for garnish. In a blender, mix vinegar and mustard. While blender is running, pour in olive oil in a steady stream; cover and blend on high speed to combine. Add the egg yolks and blend for 1 minute until the yolk is mixed into dressing. Add salt and pepper to taste. Drain the hearts of palm and toss with vinegar-mustard mixture. Cover and chill for 1 hour. To serve, arrange lettuce cups on individual salad plates and top with dressed hearts of palm. Sprinkle with julienned egg white and garnish further with salad greens in season.

Chef's note: Salted red eggs are found in Filipino, Chinese or Asian food stores. At times they are also sold natural and uncolored.

WATERCRESS, BEANSPROUT AND AVOCADO SALAD WITH CILANTRO-SESAME DRESSING

Serves 4

1 bunch watercress
1 cup beansprouts
1 whole ripe avocado, seeded and sliced

Dressing:

1/2 cup vegetable oil
6 tablespoons rice wine vinegar
1 tablespoon sugar
1 teaspoon salt
1 teaspoon ground black pepper
1 teaspoon sesame oil
2 teaspoons fresh cilantro or coriander, chopped

Toss watercress and beansprouts in large bowl. Arrange on individual salad plates and garnish with avocado slices; chill. To make dressing, combine vegetable oil, vinegar, sugar, salt, pepper and sesame oil in a medium-sized jar with a fitted lid. Shake mixture vigorously until combined; set aside and chill. To serve, add chopped cilantro or coriander to jar of dressing and shake until well mixed. Serve with salad.

BITTER MELON (*Ampalaya*) SALAD

Serves 4

2 bitter melons (*ampalaya*), split lengthwise and sliced diagonally into 1/4-inch strips
1 1/2 tablespoons salt
2 tablespoons fresh lemon juice
1/4 teaspoon pepper
1 large tomato, sliced
1 small onion, sliced into thin rings

Place sliced bitter melon (*ampalaya*) in large bowl and toss with salt; let stand for 10 minutes. Squeeze bitter melons to extract excess liquid; discard liquid. Toss bitter melon with lemon juice and pepper. Place on a serving platter. Garnish with tomatoes and onions.

Bitter Melon Salad

LOBSTER AUX FRUITS

Serves 4

4 fresh lobsters (approximately 1 1/4 pound each)
1 whole medium ripe mango, peeled, seeded, sliced
1 whole small red apple, peeled, seeded, sliced
2 whole pieces kiwi, peeled and sliced
8 fresh or canned whole lychees, peeled and seeded
other fruits of your choice
***nori* (dried seaweed) slivers**

Dressing:

2/3 cup light mayonnaise
2 tablespoons celery stalks, minced
2 tablespoons wasabi powder mixed with 2 tablespoons water
2 teaspoons lemon juice

Separate lobster tails from the claws. With kitchen scissors or a sharp knife carefully remove meat from the tails. Crack the claws with a nutcracker and remove meat as well. Cut meat into bite size pieces. Reserve roe if any. Crumble lobster roe or press through sieve. Combine with lobster and set aside. In a platter or serving plate arrange fruit slices in a fan leaving room in the center for the lobster. To make dressing, mix the mayonnaise, minced celery stalks, the dissolved wasabi powder and lemon juice. Toss lobster meat with dressing and spoon into the middle of the plate. Sprinkle top of salad with nori slivers.

CRAB AND MANGO SALAD

1/3 cup light mayonnaise
1/2 teaspoon rice wine vinegar
1/2 teaspoon sweet pickle juice
1/2 teaspoon dijon mustard
pinch of sugar
1 pound shelled crab meat, cooked
1/4 cup scallions, sliced
1 tablespoon red bell pepper, diced
1/2 teaspoon salt
1/4 teaspoon pepper
1 whole ripe mango, seeded and diced

Serves 4

In medium bowl, stir together mayonnaise, vinegar, pickle juice, mustard and sugar until blended. Add crab meat, scallions, red pepper, salt and pepper; toss lightly. Fold in diced mango. Cover and refrigerate for 30 minutes.

Chef's Note: If desired, garnish with additional mango slices.

PICKLED VEGETABLES WITH QUAIL EGGS

6 cups watercress leaves, loosely packed
10 quail eggs, hardboiled
2 cups cider vinegar
1 tablespoon sugar
1 tablespoon coarse or Kosher salt
1 tablespoon garlic, minced
3 to 5 small hot chilis
20 black peppercorns

Serves 4 to 6

In a large jar (approximately 16 ounces), place watercress and quail eggs. In a large glass measuring cup, combine vinegar, sugar, salt , garlic, chilis and peppercorns; stir until salt and sugar dissolve. Pour into bottle with quail eggs and watercress. Cover and refrigerate for 3 days, stirring occasionally. Serve chilled or at room temperature.

Crab and Mango Salad

Ensalada Filipina with Thick Garlic Dressing

ENSALADA FILIPINA WITH THICK GARLIC DRESSING

Serves 4

3/4 cup eggplant, peeled and sliced
1/2 cup garlic cloves, peeled and crushed
1/2 cup light olive oil
1/2 cup rice wine vinegar
1/2 cup clarified chicken stock
1 teaspoon salt
1/4 teaspoon pepper
1/4 head iceberg lettuce, cut into 1-inch pieces
1/4 head Romaine lettuce, cut into 1-inch pieces
2 cups tomato, chopped
2 hard boiled eggs, sliced

Blanch eggplant for 1 minute; drain and set aside. In a large jar with fitted lid, combine garlic cloves, oil, rice wine vinegar, chicken stock, salt and pepper; shake vigorously and chill until ready to serve. In a large salad bowl, arrange in layers starting with iceberg lettuce, eggplant, Romaine lettuce, tomatoes and hard boiled eggs. Cover and chill salad for at least 1 hour. To serve, remove garlic cloves from dressing mixture, screw on lid and shake vigorously. Drizzle dressing over prepared salad. Toss well to coat. Transfer salad to serving plates and serve immediately.

MUSTARD GREENS SALAD

Serves 4

1 pound mustard greens
2 tablespoons coarse or Kosher salt
1/2 cup rice wine vinegar
1/4 teaspoon black pepper

Separate stems from mustard leaves, discard stems. Wash leaves and drain. Cut the leaves into small pieces, blanch, and place in a bowl. Sprinkle with 1 tablespoon of salt and squeeze out excess water. In another bowl, toss the leaves with remaining salt, vinegar and pepper. Let stand for 30 minutes, then serve.

TOME
TOME
2
TOME
3
TOME

Native Lettuce Greens with Milkfish Salad

FIDDLEHEAD FERNS WITH GINGER AND COCONUT

Serves 4

- **1 pound fiddlehead ferns, or thin asparagus, trimmed and cut into 2-inch lengths**
- **4 cloves garlic, minced**
- **1/2-inch piece ginger, peeled and sliced into 4 rounds**
- **2 tablespoons vegetable oil**
- **1/2 cup onion, chopped**
- **1/3 cup shrimp (approximately 6 medium shrimp), peeled, deveined and chopped**
- **1 small green pepper, seeded and chopped**
- **1/2 cup coconut cream**
- **2 teaspoons fish sauce (*patis*)**
- **1/4 teaspoon pepper**

Briefly boil fiddlehead ferns (or asparagus) in lightly salted water until bright green and slightly tender. Drain and immerse in bowl of ice water to stop cooking; drain again. In large skillet, over medium heat, saute garlic and ginger in vegetable oil for 30 seconds. Add onions and saute until tender. Add shrimp and cook, stirring until pink, about 1 minute. Stir in fiddlehead ferns (or asparagus), green pepper and coconut cream. Season with fish sauce (*patis*) and black pepper. Serve immediately.

NATIVE LETTUCE GREENS WITH MILKFISH SALAD

Serves 4 to 6

1/2 + 2 tablespoons onion, chopped and divided
2 tablespoons chopped carrot
4 black peppercorns
1 cup water
1 pound milkfish or red snapper filet
4 1/2 cups romaine lettuce, shredded
2 cups tomatoes, chopped
croutons (optional), for garnish

Dressing:

1/2 cup lemon juice
1/4 cup light olive oil
2 tablespoons sugar
2 teaspoons garlic, minced
1/2 teaspoon salt
Pinch of white pepper

In a medium saucepan, over medium heat, combine 2 tablespoons chopped onion, carrot, peppercorns and water. Bring mixture to a boil and simmer 5 minutes until vegetables are tender. Add fish. Cover and cook for 5-6 minutes or until fish is opaque in color and center flakes easily. Remove fish from liquid and strain cooking liquid, reserving 1/4 cup. When fish is cool enough to handle, flake fish with fork and set aside in a medium sized bowl. In a large salad bowl, spread a third of the lettuce in the bottom of the bowl, then sprinkle with a third of the tomatoes, onion and fish. Repeat layers until the last layer is of fish; cover and chill 1 hour. Meanwhile, in a 12-ounce jar with fitted lid, combine lemon juice, olive oil, sugar, garlic, salt and pepper. Cover jar and shake vigorously and chill 1 hour. To serve, shake dressing and drizzle over prepared salad. Toss until salad ingredients are well coated and transfer immediately into salad plates. Garnish with croutons, as desired.

Chef's note: Fresh or frozen milkfish may be found in Chinese or Asian markets, grocers and other specialty food stores.

DEBBIE'S CHICKEN SALAD

Serves 2 to 4

1 1/2 cups shredded and cooked chicken breasts
1/2 cup carrots, julienned
1/4 cup scallions, sliced
1 cup cucumber, julienned
1/2 cup bean sprouts
2 tablespoons fresh cilantro, chopped

Dressing:
1/4 cup corn oil
2 tablespoons sesame oil
1 tablespoon light soy sauce
1 tablespoon hoisin sauce
1 tablespoon rice wine vinegar
Lettuce leaves for garnish

In a large bowl, toss chicken, carrots, scallions, cucumber, bean sprouts and cilantro. To make dressing, whisk together corn and sesame oils, soy sauce, hoisin sauce and rice wine vinegar in a small bowl. Pour over salad and toss. Serve on a bed of lettuce leaves.

Chef's Note: This can be served warm or cold.

FISH & SEAFOOD

In the Philippines, fish is a widely used ingredient in soups, appetizers and main dishes. For a great number of Filipinos, it remains the chief supplier of protein. It is also the source of *patis*, the popular sauce that is an indispensible ingredient and flavoring agent in Philippine cooking.

Fishing remains an important source of livelihood for a number of Filipinos. Milkfish, a national favorite, is raised mainly in ponds. This bony fish with a delicate flavor is not found in North America; but is now exported to the United States and available frozen in Filipino grocery stores.

Philippine waters abound with innumerable varieties of fish. There is also a rich supply of lobsters and crabs, as well as giant river prawns and an unusually large selection of shrimp.

< *Scallops with Lime (Dayap)-Orange Hollandaise Sauce*

ROUND SCROD FILLET WITH WARM HERBED VINAIGRETTE

Serves 4

1 1/2 pounds scrod fillets, 6 ounces each
1 tablespoon fresh herbs (basil, oregano and thyme), chopped
1/2 cup olive oil
salt and pepper to taste
1 1/2 tablespoons calamansi or lemon juice

Vinaigrette:

8 tablespoons calamansi or lemon juice
3/4 cup olive oil
1 tablespoon fresh herbs (as above), chopped
salt and pepper to taste

Marinate fish for 2 hours in herbs, oil, salt, pepper and calamansi or lemon juice. In a skillet, over medium heat, gently transfer the fillets. Cover and simmer until cooked through, 7-10 minutes, depending on thickness of fish fillets. Gently transfer fish to a platter. Keep warm. Whisk together the vinaigrette ingredients. Heat slightly to warm (about 1-2 minutes). Spoon over fish and serve at once.

Chef's note: Usual cooking time for fish, one-inch thick at thickest portion of fish, is approximately 10 minutes.

SCALLOPS WITH LIME (DAYAP)-ORANGE HOLLANDAISE SAUCE

Serves 4-6

1/2 cup unsalted butter
1/8 teaspoon salt
1/8 teaspoon ground white pepper
3 tablespoons white wine
2 cups water
1 1/2 pounds bay scallops (if using sea scallops slice horizontally)
2 cups dayap (lime)-orange hollandaise sauce (recipe follows)
parsley sprigs, for garnish

Hollandaise Sauce:

1 cup unsalted butter, melted
6 large egg yolks
2 tablespoons dayap (lime) juice
1/2 tablespoon dayap (lime) peel, grated
1 tablespoon orange peel, grated
1 tablespoon orange juice
1 tablespoon apricot brandy
1/4 teaspoon salt
1/8 teaspoon ground white pepper
1/4 teaspoon cayenne powder

In a large sauce pan, combine butter, salt, pepper, wine and water. Bring to a boil. Add scallops, reduce heat to medium, cover and cook 2-3 minutes until scallops are opaque in the center. Drain off liquid, keeping a small amount. Season scallops with remaining salt and pepper if desired, and keep warm in pan. For the sauce, melt butter in a small saucepan and reserve. In a medium saucepan, bring 2 cups of water to boil; reduce heat to simmer. Place medium glass or stainless steel bowl over simmering water (water should not touch bottom of bowl). Add egg yolks and whisk until foamy. Add lime juice, lime peel, orange peel, orange juice, brandy, salt, pepper and cayenne. Whisk vigorously until mixture is smooth and thickened, taking care not to overcook or the yolk-mixture will curdle; remove bowl from saucepan. While whisking yolk mixture, drizzle in melted butter; whisk until butter is well incorporated. Season with additional salt and pepper if desired. Keep warm and set aside. To serve, pour prepared hollandaise over the scallops. Garnish with parsley sprigs and serve immediately.

Chef's note: If sauce separates or becomes too thick, whisk in drops of hot water until smooth. "Dayap" (native lime) is a very small lime variety with a round shape that is highly aromatic and is used extensively in traditional Philippine sauces, custards and desserts.

BANANA LEAF-WRAPPED AND STEAMED PRAWNS (*Pinais na Sugpo*)

Serves 4

1 pound prawns or jumbo white shrimp
2 tablespoons *calamansi* or lemon juice
1/2 teaspoon salt
1 medium onion, sliced
2 large tomatoes, sliced
1/2 cup spring onions, chopped
enough banana leaves cut into 6 x 6–inch squares for wrapping
toothpicks or string to secure
10 pieces *calamansi*, cut in halves (or lemon, cut in wedges)
cooked rice (1 cup per person)

Peel and devein prawns or shrimp. Season with calamansi or lemon juice and salt. Marinate for 1 hour. Place a slice of onion, tomato and some spring onion on top of each prawn or shrimp and wrap in banana leaf square. Wrap each piece envelope-fashion, tucking in end, roll and secure with a toothpick or tie with a piece of string. Repeat until all the prawns are used. In a medium saucepot or steamer, arrange the wrapped prawns or shrimp. Add just enough water and steam for 5-10 minutes. Serve with calamansi or lemon with freshly cooked rice.

BAKED STUFFED POMPANO
(*Pinaputok na Pampano*)

Serves 2

1/2 cup tomatoes, diced
1/2 cup onions, diced
juice of 2 lemons
2 tablespoons shrimp paste (*bagoong*) or anchovy paste
1 whole fresh pompano, about 1 1/2 to 2 pounds, scaled and gutted
coarse or Kosher salt to taste
pepper to taste

Preheat oven to 475° F.

In a medium sized bowl, combine tomatoes, onions, lemon juice and shrimp or anchovy paste (*bagoong*). Season pompano with salt and pepper to taste. Place the fish in a roasting pan lined with aluminum foil. Stuff stomach and coat the fish with the tomato mixture. Seal with aluminum foil and bake 15-20 minutes or until fish comes out clean when flaked with a fork. Allow to stand for 5 minutes and serve.

Chef's note: Pompano can be substituted with any firm white-fleshed fish such as tilapia, sea bass or red snapper. Bagoong (shrimp paste) is found in Filipino or Asian food stores or specialty food sections of supermarkets.

FISH SLICES IN RICE WINE SAUCE

Serves 2 to 4

6 shitake mushrooms, dried
1/2 cup warm water
1 cup fish or chicken stock
1 teaspoon sugar
3 tablespoons rice wine, divided into 2 and 1 tablespoons
3 1/2 tablespoons corn starch
1/2 teaspoon salt
1 pound white fish fillets
1 egg white
1 1/4-inch piece ginger, peeled and cut into thin slices
1/2 cup peanut oil
1 tablespoon garlic, minced
1/4 cup scallions, thinly sliced
1 tablespoon fresh ginger, minced
fresh coriander or cilantro sprigs for garnish

In a small bowl, soak mushrooms in warm water for 20 minutes and drain. In a medium bowl, stir together the stock, sugar, 2 tablespoons rice wine, 1 1/2 teaspoons corn starch and salt; set aside. Cut the fish fillets into squares, measuring approximately 2 X 2 inches. In a medium bowl, whisk together the egg white, ginger slices, salt and remaining rice wine and corn starch. Add the fish to the bowl and toss, coating well. Cover and chill for 1 hour. In a large skillet, heat the oil over medium heat. Drain fish squares and carefully add to skillet. Shallow fry until golden brown, about 2 minutes on each side. Drain fish on paper towels and keep warm. Remove all but 1 tablespoon of the peanut oil from the skillet. Over medium heat, stir-fry the garlic, scallions and ginger for about 30 seconds. Add the mushrooms and stir-fry another 30 seconds. Stir in the stock mixture and cook for 2-3 minutes until sauce is thickened and will coat the back of a wooden spoon. To serve, spoon the sauce into individual serving dishes, divide fish squares evenly and place on top of sauce. Garnish with fresh coriander or cilantro sprigs. Serve immediately.

PRAWNS AND FISH ROULADE IN SAFFRON BEURRE BLANC

Serves 4

4 cups water
6 parsley stems, tied into a knot
1/4 cup onion, chopped
4 peppercorns
1 tablespoon white wine vinegar
4 large shrimp, peeled and deveined
4 fillets of sole, 6 to 8 ounces each
4 large fresh tamarind or spinach leaves
salt and pepper to taste

Saffron Beurre Blanc:

1/8 teaspoon saffron threads
2 tablespoons shallots, chopped
1/4 cup rice wine vinegar
1/4 cup Chardonnay or similar white wine
1/4 cup fish stock or clam broth
6 ounces unsalted butter, cut into small pieces and softened at room temperature
salt and pepper to taste

In a large saucepan, combine 4 cups water, parsley stems, onion, peppercorns and vinegar; bring to a boil. Reduce heat and simmer 5 minutes. Add shrimp and blanch 1 minute; remove with slotted spoon and drain on paper toweling (reserve cooking liquid). To assemble roulades, season 1 side of fillet with salt and pepper to taste. Wrap a shrimp in tamarind or spinach leaf and place at end of each fillet, seasoned side up. Roll fillet around shrimp and secure carefully with toothpicks. Repeat with remaining fillets, leaves and shrimp. Bring broth to a simmer and place roulades in saucepan. Cook covered, over medium heat for 2-3 minutes until fish is cooked through. Drain roulades on paper towel and set aside. To make sauce, combine the saffron, shallots, vinegar, wine and fish stock in a medium saucepan. Bring to a boil, then reduce to 2 tablespoons of liquid; remove from heat. When the liquid is tepid, whisk in small pieces of the butter, moving the pan on and off heat at low setting so that the butter is thick

and creamy but not melted. Continue whisking until the sauce is thick and creamy. Add salt and pepper to taste. To serve, place each roulade on a warm serving plate. Pour sauce over roulade or serve on the side.

Chef's note: Flounder or any small white fleshed fish like turbot or halibut may be substituted. The original recipe here calls for kasubha or the dried crocus of cassava flower, which differentiates itself from the sharp scents of saffron. Kasubha presents a highly sharp cheesy flavor. In the beurre blanc sauce, the acid agent originally used was green tamarind puree. In this recipe, the rice vinegar was used as a substitute.

SEAFOOD STEW WITH CORIANDER

Serves 4 to 6

1/2 pound small clams in shells
1/2 pound mussels in shells
1 tablespoon cornstarch or cornmeal
1 tablespoon vegetable oil
1/2 cup onion, diced
1 cup tomato, seeded, peeled and diced
6 cloves garlic, minced
2 slices quarter-inch size fresh ginger
4 cups chicken broth
1/2 cup clam juice
1/2 pound squid, cleaned with ink sacs removed, and cut into 1/2-inch slices
1/2 pound shrimp, peeled and deveined
2 teaspoons fresh coriander or cilantro, chopped

Clean the clams and mussels, leaving them in their shells. Place in a large bowl of water. Sprinkle with 1 tablespoon cornstarch or cornmeal (to release dirt). Let stand 1 hour; rinse and drain. Heat oil in a soup pot. Saute onion until tender, about 3 minutes. Stir in tomato and cook for 5 minutes. Stir in garlic, ginger, broth and clam juice. Heat to a boil. Add squid and cook gently until tender, about 3 minutes. Add remaining seafood, cover and simmer for an additional 3 minutes. Sprinkle with 2 teaspoons chopped coriander or cilantro and serve.

FISH BISQUE WITH PUFF PASTRY

(*Sinigang Bisque with Puff Pastry*)

Serves 4

1 sheet puff pastry
2 cloves garlic, minced
2 tablespoons olive oil
3 tablespoons all-purpose flour
8 cups water
1 cup half-and-half cream or heavy cream
1/2 cup onion, chopped
1/4 cup leeks, chopped
2 sprigs fresh dill
1/4 cup lemon juice
1 teaspoon peppercorns
1 cup clam juice
1 1/2 pounds fish heads
salt to taste

Cut 4 rounds of puff pastry just larger than the tops of the soup cups or bowls; bake accordingly to package directions or until golden brown. In heavy bottomed soup pot, over medium heat, saute garlic in olive oil until light brown, about 2 minutes. Add flour and cook, stirring constantly for approximately 2 minutes (flour should not turn brown). Stir in water and half-and-half, and cook for 5 minutes, stirring constantly. Add the vegetables, dill, lemon juice, peppercorns, clam juice and fish heads. Simmer 45 minutes uncovered until desired thickness is achieved. Skim soup, remove fish heads to plate and strain the soup. Season soup with salt to taste. Collect meat from fish heads and divide among individual soup cups; pour bisque into cups. Top each with prepared puff pastry.

Chef's note: Brush egg wash (beaten whole egg with a little water) over puff pastry rounds before baking. Bake until golden brown. Serve hot from oven.

- 1 1/2 pounds medium shrimp
- 2 tablespoons olive oil
- 2-3 cloves garlic, minced
- 2 tablespoons onion, chopped
- 1/2 cup coconut milk, unsweetened
- 1/4 teaspoon pepper
- 1/2 teaspoon salt
- 2 tablespoons fresh chilis, chopped
- 1 teaspoon ginger, minced

SHRIMP IN COCONUT MILK

Serves 4

Peel fresh shrimp and clean thoroughly. Set aside. Heat oil in pan and saute garlic and onion until brown. Add shrimp and saute 4 to 5 minutes until pink and cooked through. Pour in coconut milk and season with pepper and salt to taste. At the last minute, add chilis and ginger. Serve immediately.

Chef's note: Unsweetened coconut milk can be bought canned in 12 ounce containers in Asian specialty food shops or Hispanic food sections of supermarkets. Dilute with 3 to 4 parts water until liquid is thin. Or make coconut milk, mixing coconut powder and water.

WINGED BEANS (*Sigadillas*) WITH SHRIMP

Serves 4

- **2 tablespoon vegetable oil**
- **6 cloves garlic, minced**
- **1 cup onion, diced**
- **2/3 cup shrimp, cleaned and diced**
- **8 winged beans or 16 string beans, halved lengthwise**
- **1/4 teaspoon oregano, dried**
- **fresh black pepper to taste**
- **fish sauce (*patis*) to taste**
- **2-3 tablespoons walnuts, shelled and chopped (optional)**

In a small skillet, heat oil. Saute garlic until light brown. Add onion and cook until tender. Add shrimp and cook until pink. Add beans and cook until tender, about 3-5 minutes. Season with oregano, black pepper and fish sauce to taste. Sprinkle walnuts on top as desired. Serve immediately.

Chef's note: the Winged Bean is a relative new comer to the United States. Grown in Florida it is also known as Asparagus Pea. It consists of a stem and four delicate fins. It can be cut horizontally into stars then blanched, braised or stir fried. Winged Beans are seasonal (available only in the summer), but the Oriental long beans or regular string beans can be used as substitutes as shown here.

STEAMED GROUPER (*Lapu-Lapu*) WITH VEGETABLE JULIENNE

Serves 4

1 tablespoon orange peel, grated
1 teaspoon ginger, grated
1 tablespoon lime peel, grated
2 teaspoons sesame oil
1 1/2 cups fish stock
1 1/2 tablespoons garlic, minced
6 tablespoons unsalted butter
2 tablespoons chopped fresh cilantro
4 grouper (*lapu-lapu*) fillets, about 6 ounces each
salt and pepper to taste
1 tablespoon of each of the following: orange peel, lime peel, celery, leeks, carrots, ginger, sliced julienne style
8 tablespoons walnut oil

Garlic Herbed Butter:

1/2 cup unsalted butter
1 tablespoon chopped garlic
parsley, basil, coriander

In a large skillet, place grated orange, ginger, lime, sesame oil and fish stock. Bring to a boil, reduce heat, cover and simmer for 5 minutes. Meanwhile, in a large skillet, saute garlic in butter until golden brown. Stir in chopped cilantro, remove from heat and keep warm. Season fish filets with salt and pepper to taste. Add to pan with simmering water, cover with julienned vegetables and citrus peel. Drizzle the walnut oil over the filets. Cover and simmer over medium heat 4-5 minutes until fish is opaque in center. Carefully remove fish and julienned vegetables with slotted spatula. Place on warm serving plates. Make garlic butter by sauteeing garlic in melted butter until golden brown. Add herbs. To serve, pour warm garlic herbed butter over fillets.

MEATS & POULTRY

The early Filipinos ate deer, pig and several other varieties of game. The Spaniards introduced beef to the Philippines but the raising of cattle for consumption did not become important until the arrival of the beef-loving Americans. Today, a few provinces raise cattle, but most of the beef is still imported from Australia and New Zealand. Pork is quite popular. The most important pork dish remains the *lechon*, a whole suckling pig roasted over coals and served with the traditional liver sauce. *Lechon* is a favorite for fiestas and official functions.

Chicken, formerly used widely in sacrificial ceremonies, is now commonly used in many recipes. It lends itself to Malay as well as Spanish inspired dishes and remains a favorite among Filipinos. Max's Fried Chicken is an institution in the Philippines. Another particular favorite is the *Nilagang Manok*- boiled chicken cooked with a melange of vegetables. There is also a bountiful supply of quails, wild boar, wild duck, deer and snipes to be found in the islands.

< *Roast Chicken with Passionfruit Sauce*

BEER BRAISED LAMB STEW

Serves 4

2 pounds stewing lamb, cubed
2 teaspoons green peppercorns, mashed
1/2 teaspoon cumin, ground
salt to taste
freshly ground black pepper
4 tablespoons olive oil, divided, plus additional if needed
1 cup onion, chopped
5 cloves garlic, minced
2 bottles (12 ounces each) San Miguel Beer (other beer brands may be substituted)
2 cups beef broth or lamb stock
4 small red potatoes, cubed (1 3/4 cups)
2 carrots, peeled and cubed (1 cup)
1/2 cup green peas
1 tablespoon cilantro or coriander, chopped
freshly cooked wild rice, approximately 4 cups

On a piece of waxed paper, toss lamb with peppercorns and cumin. Season with salt and pepper. In a large, heavy-bottomed soup pot, over high heat, heat oil until almost smoking. Brown meat, in 2 batches, about 5 minutes for each batch. Add more oil if necessary. Remove meat with slotted spoon to plate. Reduce heat to medium and add 2 tablespoons of oil to the pot. Add onions and garlic and saute until tender. Return lamb and any juices to pot. Stir in beer and broth. Simmer, uncovered, until tender but firm, about 1 1/2 hours, skimming occasionally. Add potatoes and carrots and cook covered, for another 20 minutes until tender. Stir in peas and sprinkle with cilantro or coriander. Serve with the cooked rice.

ROAST CHICKEN WITH PASSIONFRUIT SAUCE

Serves 2 to 4

1 whole roasting chicken (3 1/2 pounds)
2 tablespoons mixed herbs (sage, thyme, chervil)
salt and pepper to taste
2 tablespoons butter, melted
1/2 cup chicken stock, divided
1 teaspoon cornstarch
1/4 cup orange juice
2 tablespoons white wine
8 passionfruit, pulp strained to extract 1/4 cup juice
orange segments and passion fruit halves, for garnish

Preheat oven to 325° F.

Rub the chicken (including inside cavity) with mixed herbs, salt and pepper. Roast chicken, basting occasionally with the melted butter and drippings from the roasting pan, about 1 1/4 hours or until juices run clear when the thigh joint is pierced with a knife. Let chicken sit 15 minutes before carving. Meanwhile, in a small-size bowl, mix 1 tablespoon chicken stock and 1 teaspoon cornstarch; set aside. In a saucepan combine remaining chicken stock, orange juice, white wine and passionfruit juice. Over medium heat, simmer sauce until slightly reduced and flavorful; about 10 minutes. Stir in cornstarch mixture and simmer briefly until thickened; remove from heat and season with salt and pepper to taste. To serve, garnish chicken with orange segments and passion fruit halves and serve with passionfruit sauce.

BEEF TENDERLOIN IN PAPAYA SEED SAUCE

Serves 4 to 6

3 tablespoons unsalted butter, softened and divided
3 tablespoons of the following mixed dried herbs: thyme, oregano and rosemary
1/2 teaspoon salt
1/2 teaspoon pepper
2 tablespoons vegetable oil
2 pounds beef tenderloin, trimmed
1/2 cup red wine

Sauce:

4 tablespoons butter, divided
1/4 cup onion, chopped
1/4 cup carrot, diced into 1/4-inch pieces
1/4 cup celery, chopped
trimmings from the tenderloin
2 tablespoons all-purpose flour
1/2 cup red wine
4 cups beef broth or stock, divided
1 cup fresh papaya seeds
salt and pepper to taste

Preheat oven to 300° F.

In a small bowl, stir together 2 tablespoons of the butter, the dried herbs, salt and pepper to form a paste. Rub on tenderloin and coat well. In a large skillet, over high heat, sear tenderloin fillet in2 tablespoons vegetable oil until all sides are brown. Transfer tenderloin to a roasting pan and roast to desired degree of doneness; reserve juices in skillet. Over medium heat, add the wine to the juices in skillet and stir with a wooden spoon to dissolve any browned material, bringing liquid to a boil, while stirring. To make the sauce, heat 2 tablespoons butter in a large saucepan over medium heat. Saute onions, carrots and celery until soft, about 4 minutes. Add any trimmings from the tenderloin and saute until brown. Sprinkle with 2 tablespoons flour and stir until dissolved. Pour in the red wine and boil until reduced by half, about 5 minutes. Add the remaining beef stock and papaya seeds. Bring to a boil, lower heat and simmer for 30 minutes until sauce has developed a rich flavor and is slightly thickened. Strain the sauce into a medium bowl, pushing contents with a wooden spoon to extract liquid. Discard strained solids and return sauce to saucepan. Over low heat, stir in remaining

2 tablespoons butter until melted and sauce has a nice sheen; keep warm. To serve, let tenderloin stand 10 minutes and slice. Serve with the sauce and buttered vegetables.

Chef's note: Fresh papaya seeds give off a piquant and peppery flavor, as well as, contain tenderizing properties. Serve this dish with boiled fettucini on the side. Follow boiling instructions for 1 16-ounce package of dried fettucini; drain and keep warm. Hint: Pour a tablespoon of olive oil through the fettucini to keep from sticking and to give the pasta a nice shine. Use tri-colored peppercorns to give added color if desired.

CHICKEN PASOLO

Serves 4 to 6

1 whole chicken (about 3 pounds) cut into pieces
3 medium onions, peeled and quartered
2 potatoes, peeled and quartered
2 leeks, greens trimmed to 1-inch, white rinsed well and cut into 3-inch pieces
2 links chorizo sausage (Bilbao type), cut into pieces
6 slices (1/4-inch each) Canadian bacon, cut into pieces
2 tablespoons whole peppercorns
Approximately 3 cups water
banana leaves to cover clay cooking pot

Place chicken, onions, potatoes, leeks, chorizo, Canadian bacon and peppercorns in clay pot. Add 3 cups or more boiling water to bring water level up to one inch from rim. Cover pot with banana leaves, tucking leaves inside pot to cover chicken and vegetables. Cover with lid. Place on large sheet or roasting pan. Place in cold oven and turn thermostat to 450° F. Cook 50-60 minutes or until chicken is cooked and juices run clear when meat is pierced with knife. Remove chicken, vegetables, chorizo and bacon to a platter. Cover chicken, vegetables and broth and chill 1 to 2 days. Remove any fat congealed on surface of broth. To serve, reheat chicken, vegetables, chorizo and bacon in broth and serve together in casserole dish.

BEEF SHORT RIBS IN MONGO

Serves 6 to 8

- **2 pounds beef short ribs, cut between bones and into 2-inch pieces**
- **4 cups water**
- **1 1/2 cups beef broth**
- **1 tablespoon corn oil**
- **1 tablespoon garlic, minced**
- **1/4 cup onion, chopped**
- **1 1/2 tablespoons *bagoong alamang* (baby shrimp paste)**
- **1 cup mongo beans (dried mung beans)**
- **3 1/2 cups beef broth (use cooking liquid from beef ribs)**
- **1 1/2 tablespoons *patis* (fish sauce)**
- **3/4 teaspoon ground pepper**
- **2 cups fresh leafy green vegetables (spinach, pepper leaves or as preferred)**

In a large soup pot, boil ribs covered in water and beef broth for 1 1/2 hours. Skim fat from broth; set ribs and broth aside. In a large heavy-bottomed soup pot, heat oil over medium heat; saute garlic and onions until transparent, then stir in *bagoong*. Add the mongo beans and the reserved broth and cook for 20 minutes. Stir in the *patis* and pepper; add the short ribs and simmer until ribs are warmed through. Add leafy green vegetables, about 2 cups; continue stirring for one minute. Serve immediately.

Chef's note: Dried mongo or mung beans are small legume beans available in Asian specialty sections and food stores, as well as in health food stores. They vary from green to yellow varieties; the green being most common and popular. Lentils may be substituted here. The dried beans must be soaked in warm water overnight, then cooked in a soup pot for 20-40 minutes until tender. Portion 1 cup dried beans and cook in 4 cups water. Other substitutes for fresh leafy green vegetables are Swiss chard and Chinese watercress. Bagoong (baby shrimp paste) is found in Asian specialty stores and the gourmet section of food stores.

CHICKEN STEAK WITH BEANSPROUTS

Serves 4

1/2 cup soy sauce
2 tablespoons sugar
3 tablespoons lemon juice
4 chicken cutlets boneless and skinless
2 tablespoons unsalted butter
2 tablespoons vegetable oil
1 cup onions, sliced
2 cups beansprouts
1 sweet red pepper, julienned
1 green or yellow pepper, julienned

In a shallow bowl, mix soy sauce, sugar and lemon juice. Add chicken, turning over to coat in marinade. Cover and chill 1 hour. In a large skillet, saute marinated chicken (reserve marinade) in butter over medium heat, until golden on both sides, about 4 minutes. Remove chicken to plate and keep warm. In a large, clean skillet, heat 2 tablespoons vegetable oil until very hot; add onions, beansprouts and peppers. Stir fry 3 minutes until vegetables are tender. Pour in 1/4 cup of reserved marinade and cook, stirring, until marinade boils. Arrange stir-fried vegetables on platter and top with chicken.

LAMB IN MUSTARD CRUST WITH BANANA BLOSSOM SAUCE

Serves 6

1/4 cup + 1 tablespoon Dijon mustard, divided
1 tablespoon rosemary, dried
1 tablespoon thyme, dried
1/2 teaspoon salt, divided
1/2 + 1/8 teaspoon pepper
3/4 cup all-purpose flour
1/4 cup + 2 tablespoons butter, divided
1 tablespoon vegetable oil
3 pounds lamb roast (cut from a boneless leg or shoulder, rolled and tied)
1 egg, beaten
1 can (13 3/4 ounces) beef broth
1/2 cup + 1 tablespoon Port wine, divided
1/4 cup dried banana blossoms
2 1/2 teaspoons cornstarch

Preheat oven to 450° F.

In a small bowl, combine 1/4 cup mustard, rosemary, thyme, 1/4 teaspoon salt and 1/2 teaspoon pepper to form a paste; set aside. In a medium-size bowl, combine flour, 1/4 cup butter, remaining mustard, 1/4 teaspoon salt and 1/8 teaspoon pepper; with fork, work mixture into a fine streusel; set aside. In a large heavy skillet, heat oil until almost smoking. Brown lamb on all sides, about 8 minutes. Remove lamb onto a plate. Using a pastry brush, brush lamb with egg. Brush mustard mixture on lamb to coat evenly. Return lamb to skillet and top with streusel mixture. Roast lamb for 10 minutes, then lower heat to 400° F and roast for 20-25 minutes until rare, or longer until desired doneness is reached. Meanwhile in a saucepan, bring broth, 1/2 cup Port and banana blossoms to a boil, simmer for 10 minutes. In a small bowl, stir together 1 tablespoon Port and cornstarch; stir into stock mixture and simmer 1 minute until sauce thickens and coats back of a spoon. Remove from heat and whisk in 2 tablespoons butter, one tablespoon at a time, until incorporated and sauce is shiny. Season with salt and pepper

to taste. To serve, slice the lamb into fillets of desired thickness and pour hot banana blossom sauce over.

Chef's Note: Banana blossoms are available in Asian specialty food stores and gourmet grocers.

Grilled Duck with Mango-Anise Sauce

GRILLED DUCK WITH MANGO-ANISE SAUCE

Serves 4

1/4 cup red wine vinegar
1/4 cup sugar
1/4 cup water
2 tablespoons shallots, finely chopped
1 tablespoon butter + 1/2 cup butter, cut into cubes
1/2 cup beef or duck stock
1/2 ripe medium mango, peeled and pureed
salt and pepper to taste
1/4 teaspoon star-anise, ground
4 duck breasts, skin on, deboned, 6 ounces each
salt and pepper to rub on duck breasts
1 large mango divided into quarters, peeled and sliced into fans, for garnish
rosemary sprigs or other fresh herbs, for garnish

Make caramel sauce by combining the vinegar, sugar and water in a small sauce pan; boil until sugar is dissolved; set aside. In a separate pan, saute shallots in 1 tablespoon butter. Add stock and mango puree and combine with caramel sauce. Whisk in the remaining butter slowly until smooth and shiny. Season with salt, pepper and anise. Keep warm. Season duck breasts with salt and pepper. Broil skin side down, turning over, about 6 minutes per side, until medium rare. Cut into slices to arrange into a fan on plate. Spoon prepared warm sauce on plate and place on top of the sliced duck. Garnish with sliced ripe mango cut into fan shapes and sprigs of rosemary or other fresh herbs.

- **2 tablespoons soy sauce**
- **2 tablespoons sesame oil**
- **2 tablespoons *patis* (fish sauce)**
- **1 whole chicken (3 1/2 pounds)**
- **3 cups + 1 tablespoon coarse or Kosher salt, divided**
- **1 1/2 teaspoons black pepper**
- **1 medium onion, peeled and quartered**
- **1 celery stalk, cut into 1-inch pieces**

SALT-RUBBED AND STEWED CHICKEN POT (*Pinaupaung Manok*)

Serves 4 to 6

In a small bowl, stir together soy sauce, sesame oil and *patis*. Rub outside and inside of chicken with soy sauce mixture, 1 tablespoon of the coarse or Kosher salt and pepper. Stuff cavity with onion and celery. In a Dutch oven or heavy-bottomed soup pot, place remaining coarse salt and spread evenly. Place the chicken on top of the salt. Place pan over moderate heat, covered. Cook until juices run clear when thigh is pierced with tip of a knife, about 1 hour. Carefully remove chicken from pot, discarding any salt that clings to the bottom of the chicken. Cover loosely with foil and let chicken stand 10 minutes before carving.

GINGER AND SPRING ONION CHICKEN

6 chicken breasts, halved and boned with skin removed
2 eggs
1/2 cup milk
1 1/2 cups bread crumbs
1 cup all-purpose flour
1 tablespoon salt
1 teaspoon pepper
1 1/2 cups corn oil
1/4 cup ginger, minced
2/3 cup spring onions (scallions), chopped, divided
2 tablespoons soy sauce
1 tablespoon sugar
1 tablespoon corn starch, stirred into 1 tablespoon cold water
1 cup water
3/4 cup spring onion (scallions), for garnish

Serves 4 to 6

Place chicken breasts between two sheets of wax paper and pound with bottom of heavy skillet or meat mallet to flatten slightly; set aside. In a large shallow bowl, whisk egg and milk together. Place bread crumbs on sheet of waxed paper; set both aside. In a large plastic bag, combine flour, salt and pepper; shake to mix well. Add the chicken and shake to coat in flour. Remove chicken from bag and gently shake to remove excess flour. Dip in egg mixture and coat with bread crumbs. In a large skillet, heat oil over medium heat. Shallow fry chicken breasts in batches, 6-7 minutes each batch until golden brown, turn over. Drain on paper towels and keep warm. Discard all but 2 tablespoons of the oil and saute ginger and onion for 3 minutes until softened. Stir in soy sauce, sugar and cornstarch-water mixture. Simmer until thick. Strain sauce to remove ginger and onion. To serve, pour sauce over chicken breasts; sprinkle with remaining chopped spring onions (scallions).

CHICKEN IN BEER

Serves 4

- 1/4 cup light soy sauce
- 3 tablespoons lime juice
- 1/4 teaspoon pepper
- 1 whole chicken (about 3 to 3 1/2 pounds), skinned and cut into 8 pieces
- 1 medium onion (8 oz.), sliced thin
- 3 tablespoons butter, divided
- 3 cups water
- 1 cup Pilsner beer (San Miguel Negra)
- 3 medium potatoes (6 oz. each), each pared and cut into 8 pieces
- salt and pepper to taste
- 2 tablespoons fresh parsley, chopped

In a large bowl, combine soy sauce, lime juice and pepper; add chicken pieces, turning to coat; cover and marinate 1 hour, turning pieces over once. In a medium saucepan, saute onion in 1 tablespoon butter until transparent, about 6 minutes. Drain chicken pieces and add to saucepan with water. Bring to a boil over high heat and then reduce to simmer; add beer and potatoes. Cover and simmer for 15 minutes. Remove scum from the liquid. Cover and simmer for additional 15 minutes until potatoes are tender and juices from chicken run clear when pierced with knife. Drain mixture, returning broth to saucepot; keep chicken and potatoes warm. Boil broth over high heat to reduce mixture to 2 cups, about 20 minutes. Mash 1 cup of the potatoes with a fork and whisk into boiling liquid; whisk until slightly thickened. Whisk in remaining butter, one tablespoon at a time, until melted. Season with salt and pepper to taste; stir in chopped parsley. To serve, pour sauce over chicken and potatoes; serve hot.

PASTEL OF SNIPES OR QUAIL

Serves 6

1 sheet of puff pastry (approximately 1 foot square)
1 egg
2 tablespoons milk
6 ounces ham, cut into 1/2 -inch cubes
1 medium potato, cut into 1/4 -inch cubes (about 1 cup)
1/2 cup onion, peeled and chopped
24 whole white button mushrooms
1/3 cup red pepper, chopped
1/3 cup green pepper, chopped
5 tablespoons butter (unsalted)
5 tablespoons all-purpose flour
1 cup chicken stock
1 cup heavy cream
12 snipes or quail cut into pieces
1/2 teaspoon salt
1/4 teaspoon pepper
2 tablespoons cooking sherry

Preheat oven to 350° F.

On lightly floured work surface, lay out sheet of puff pastry; invert a 1 1/2 quart casserole on top of pastry and cut out shape by tracing with sharp knife around rim of dish (lightly roll pastry out first if dish is larger than sheet of pastry). Carefully shape pastry on baking sheet and chill. In a small bowl, whisk egg and milk until smooth; set aside. In a large skillet, over medium heat, sweat ham, potatoes, onion, mushrooms and peppers in butter for 5 minutes, or until potatoes are tender. Sprinkle mixture with flour and cook. Continue stirring for another 5 minutes. Add stock and bring to a boil, stirring until thickened, 3-4 minutes. Add cream and meat. Bring to a boil again and cook, stirring for another 4 minutes. Season with salt and pepper. Add sherry. Pour mixture into 1 1/2 quart casserole baking dish. Cover with chilled pastry and brush with egg-milk mixture. Place baking dish on baking sheet and bake for 20-25 minutes until filling is bubbling and pastry is golden and puffed.

Chef's note: Handle chilled pastry gently when lowering into filling. Seal pastry onto edges and brush with the egg-milk mixture. Puff pastry is available in the frozen food section of grocery stores and supermarkets. Chicken meat cut into one inch cubes can be substituted for the snipes or quail if desired.

PORK AND VEGETABLES STEWED IN TOMATO AND ANCHOVY PASTE

Serves 2 to 4

4 ounces baby eggplant, cut into 1/2-inch thick slices
4 ounces bittermelon, cut into 1/2-inch thick slices
4 ounces string beans, cut into 1/2-inch thick pieces
4 ounces okra, cut into 1/2-inch thick slices
1 tablespoon onion, sliced
2 tablespoons olive oil
1 pound boneless pork shoulder, cubed
1 teaspoon garlic, minced
1 can (8 ounces) whole tomatoes
2-3 tablespoons *bagoong* (baby shrimp or anchovy paste)
2 cups rice water (collect water from washing rice)
2 tablespoons tomato paste
1 teaspoon salt
rice wine vinegar and coarse or Kosher salt to taste

In a large soup pot, blanch the eggplant, bittermelon, string beans and okra for 5 minutes; drain and set aside. In a large skillet, saute onions in 2 tablespoons olive oil until tender. Add the pork and garlic and saute for an additional 5 minutes. Add the canned tomatoes and *bagoong* (baby shrimp or anchovy paste). Cover and cook for 15 minutes. Remove cover and stir in 2 cups of rice water, 2 tablespoons tomato paste and simmer uncovered, about 35 minutes until thickened and meat is tender. Season with salt; add vegetables and simmer briefly until vegetables are warmed through. Serve piping hot with vinegar and coarse salt on the side.

Roasted Lamb with Dayap Leaves in Guava Sauce

ROASTED LAMB WITH DAYAP LEAVES IN GUAVA SAUCE

Serves 2

2 boneless saddle lamb fillets (8 ounces each), fat trimmed
1 teaspoon dayap leaves, chopped
1/4 teaspoon thyme
salt and pepper to taste
1 tablespoon butter
1 tablespoon olive oil

Sauce:

1 1/2 cups rich brown lamb or veal stock
1/2 cup water
1/4 cup fruity red wine
2 large ripe guavas, peeled and seeded
1 teaspoon guava jelly
salt and pepper to taste
2 tablespoons unsalted butter, cut into pieces
guava preserves, for garnish

Preheat oven to 450° F.

Rub lamb fillets with chopped dayap (lime) leaves, thyme, salt and pepper. Place in glass baking dish, cover and refrigerate 1 hour. In a large skillet, melt butter and olive oil together. Over medium-high heat, sear lamb on all sides, about 5 minutes. Place skillet in the oven and roast lamb 5 minutes or more, depending on desired doneness. Remove from oven, let sit 5 minutes and slice into medallions. Meanwhile, in a large saucepan, combine the stock, water, red wine, guava fruit and guava jelly. Bring mixture to a boil and reduce to 1 cup. Transfer mixture to blender or food processor and puree. Strain sauce back into sauce pan, and thin with more stock if sauce is too thick. Season sauce with salt and pepper to taste. Bring sauce to a simmer and stir in 2 tablespoons butter until melted and sauce is shiny. Serve with the roasted lamb and garnish with guava preserves.

Chef's note: Dayap leaves are lime leaves, found in Thai food stores and Chinatown markets.

4 quails, 6-8 ounces each
2 teaspoons soy sauce
2 tablespoons olive oil
1/2 cup carrot, chopped
1/2 cup onion, chopped
3 cloves garlic, crushed
1 sprig thyme
1 sprig marjoram
1 sprig parsley
15 black peppercorns
1/4 teaspoon salt
1/4 cup *lambanog* (Philippine gin)
1/4 cup chicken broth or stock
2 tablespoons butter
1/4 cup golden raisins
Marjoram and thyme sprigs for garnish

ANGEL QUAILS IN GIN (*Lambanog*) AND RAISIN SAUCE

Serves 2

Preheat oven to 375° F.

Season quails with soy sauce. In a braising pan, heat olive oil over medium heat, arrange quails, breast side down and sprinkle with carrots, onions, garlic, herbs, black peppercorns and salt. Place in oven and roast, turning quails once and basting frequently, until skin is golden and juices run clear, about 30 minutes. Remove quails to plate and keep warm. Over medium heat, pour *lambanog* (gin) in braising pan and deglaze, stirring 1 minute. Stir in butter over medium heat until there's a shine. Stir in raisins. Season with salt and pepper to taste. Pour sauce over quails and garnish with sprigs of thyme and marjoram. Serve immediately.

Pork Roll

PORK ROLL
(Embutido)

Serves 4 to 6

1 pound ground pork
1/2 cup bacon, minced (7 ounces)
1 hot dog, minced (1/2 cup)
1/2 cup Parmesan cheese, grated
2 eggs, beaten
1/4 cup sweet pickle relish
1/4 cup red pepper, chopped
1/4 cup raisins
2 tablespoons catsup
2 tablespoons Worcestershire sauce
1 tablespoon soy sauce
1 1/2 teaspoons salt
1/4 teaspoon pepper
3 hard boiled eggs, shelled

Preheat oven to 325° F.

In a large bowl, mix all ingredients except hard boiled eggs. Place mixture in a double thickness foil sheet and form into a 9-inch loaf; press hard boiled eggs into the middle. Twist ends of foil to seal roll; place on sheet pan. Bake until internal temperature reaches 155° F, about 1 hour. Slice into 1/2-inch thick portions. Serve warm or cold as desired, with salsa or chutney.

BEEF MECHADO

Serves 4

3 stalks celery, cut into 1-inch pieces
1 two-pound piece of brisket
1/4 cup soy sauce
1 tablespoon black peppercorns, crushed
3 cloves garlic, minced
2 medium fresh tomatoes, chopped
1 medium onion, diced
1 green bell pepper, diced

Preheat oven to 350° F.

Sprinkle bottom of roasting pan with celery. Rub brisket with soy sauce, black pepper and garlic. Arrange meat on celery. Top with tomatoes, onion and green pepper. Cover with foil or top of pan. Place in the oven and bake 2 to 2 1/2 hours until tender but not falling apart. Let stand before slicing.

Chef's note: For best results, slice the meat against the grain.

2 tablespoons olive oil, divided
8 ounces fresh green papaya (1 small Hawaiian papaya), peeled, seeded and cubed
1 cup onion, peeled chopped
1 tablespoon ginger, peeled and slivered
4 chicken breasts, boneless and skinless, halved (about 1 1/2 pounds)
5 whole peppercorns
1 teaspoon *patis* (fish sauce)
2 cups chicken broth
1 teaspoon mustard seeds, toasted
1/4 cup ginger, peeled and slivered, for garnish
fresh chili leaves, for garnish

POLLO CAROLINA

Serves 4

In a heavy-bottomed soup pot, over medium heat, in 1 tablespoon of oil, saute papaya, onion and ginger until tender, about 4 minutes. Remove with slotted spoon and place in bowl; set aside. Add remaining tablespoon of oil to soup pot and saute chicken 4-5 minutes until lightly browned. Sprinkle with peppercorns, fish sauce, broth and mustard seeds. Heat to a boil and simmer until chicken is tender, about 6 minutes. Transfer chicken to a plate; keep warm. Strain contents of soup pot, reserving broth and papaya mixture. In a food processor or blender, puree papaya mixture with some of the stock until a sauce consistency is reached. Return to pan and warm briefly. Arrange chicken on a platter. Garnish with ginger and fresh chili leaves.

Chef's note: Pepper leaves or other fresh green herbs may be substituted for the chili leaves as garnish.

SMOKED CHICKEN WITH GOAT CHEESE

Serves 2 to 4

2 whole cloves of garlic, unpeeled
1 tablespoon olive oil
1/2 cup mild goat cheese (4 ounces)
1/2 cup fresh parsley, minced
2 tablespoons sweet butter, softened
1 shallot, minced
1 teaspoon each fresh rosemary and thyme, minced
1 teaspoon dried herbs de Provence
salt to taste
freshly ground black pepper
1 whole smoked chicken (1 1/2 pounds) or 3/4 pound whole smoked chicken breasts, with skin intact
2 sprigs fresh rosemary (optional)
2 sprigs fresh thyme (optional)
1 clove garlic, halved

Preheat oven to 350° F.

Rub unpeeled garlic with oil. Roast on piece of foil for 20 minutes, or until tender; peel when cool. In a medium-size bowl, mash garlic, cheese, parsley, butter, shallots, rosemary, thyme, herbs de Provence with a fork. Add salt and pepper to taste. Loosen chicken skin with fingers and spread mixture under skin. If using whole smoked chicken, add sprigs of fresh herbs to cavity. Rub whole garlic on skin (and in cavity if using whole chicken). Bake uncovered, until heated through, about 15 minutes. Serve immediately.

SHORT RIBS WITH GUAVA SAUCE

Serves 4 to 6

2 pounds beef short ribs, cut in 2 X 3-inch pieces
5 tablespoons soy sauce
3 tablespoons cider vinegar
2 tablespoons brown sugar
8 black peppercorns, crushed
1/2 cup water
1/2 cup all-purpose flour
1/2 cup olive oil

Marinate the ribs in soy sauce, vinegar, sugar and crushed pepper, 1 to 2 hours. Transfer to a heavy-bottomed pan and cook in 1/2 cup of water, adding more as needed 3/4 cup at a time), for 30 minutes or until fork tender. Place ribs on colander to

Sauce:

1/2 cup sugar
1/4 cup water
8 ripe guavas, halved
lime zest, slivered, for garnish

drain sauce/marinade. Dredge in flour and fry in oil. Meanwhile make guava sauce. Make a light syrup combining 1/2 cup sugar and 1/4 cup water in a small saucepan. Bring to a boil over medium heat and stir until sugar is dissolved. Add scooped flesh from 4 large or 8 small guavas. Cook about 10 minutes until guava is tender. Sprinkle with lime zest. Serve on the side.

Chef's note: If guavas are sweet, season with 1 to 2 tablespoons lime juice.

WHOLE STUFFED CHICKEN RELLENO

Serves 6 to 8

1 whole roasting chicken, about 4 pounds, deboned
1/4 cup + 2 tablespoons fresh lemon juice
salt and pepper, to taste
1 pound ground pork
1/2 cup Parmesan cheese, grated
1/2 cup sweet pickle relish
8 ounces chorizo, skin removed and meat chopped
2 large eggs
1 jar (4 ounces) pimiento pieces, drained
1/2 cup raisins
sliced hard boiled eggs and steamed vegetables, for garnish (optional)

Preheat oven to 350° F.

Season chicken with 2 tablespoons lemon juice, salt and pepper to taste. Refrigerate.

In a large bowl, mix pork, Parmesan cheese, relish, chorizo, eggs, pimiento and raisins. Stuff the chicken with mixture. Wrap chicken in aluminum foil and cook 1 hour or until done and pork is cooked. Remove from oven and let stand 15 minutes before removing foil. Slice crosswise and garnish with hard boiled eggs and steamed vegetables, if desired.

Chef's note: The butcher will debone the chicken upon request.

ADOBO

Adobo is considered the national dish of the Philippines. This dish consists of chunks of chicken or pork or both cooked in soy sauce, vinegar, bay leaf, lots of garlic and whole peppercorns. The stew is allowed to cook until the meats are tender and the remaining sauce slightly thickened. Some people prefer their adobos dry which may entail frying them afterwards, while others prefer them moist served in their original sauce. As a style of cooking, it can be applied to fowl, fish, shellfish and vegetables.

Another version of the adobo is made without soy sauce but with the addition of coconut milk after most of the sauce has been cooked away. This type of adobo is believed to be derived from the Malayan tradition whereas the former is of the Hispanic.

< *Chicken Adobo with Coconut Milk*

top: Hamburger Adobo, bottom: typical adobo ingredients

HAMBURGER ADOBO

Serves 4

- 1/2 pound ground round beef
- 1/2 pound ground chuck beef
- 1/4 cup onion, minced
- 2 tablespoons soy sauce
- 1 tablespoon red wine vinegar
- 4 cloves garlic, minced
- 1 teaspoon ground black pepper
- 4 hamburger buns
- tomato slices, for garnish

Mix ground round and chuck with onion, soy sauce, vinegar, garlic and pepper. Cover and let stand 1 hour. Form mixture into 4 patties, about 1 inch thick. In a hot cast iron skillet, cook hamburgers to desired doneness turning once. Serve with tomato slices on hamburger buns.

CHICKEN ADOBO PRIMAVERA

Serves 4

- 3 medium carrots, julienned
- 2 cups zucchini, sliced
- 2 cups broccoli florets
- 2 cups cauliflower florets
- 4 chicken cutlets, approximately 5 ounces each, skin removed
- 1 cup water
- 3/4 cup Balsamic vinegar
- 1/4 cup soy sauce
- 2 tablespoons garlic, minced
- 3 bay leaves, dried
- 1/2 teaspoon sugar
- 1 medium bunch watercress, stems removed (about 1 cup)
- 1 cup red tomato, diced
- 2 tablespoons red bell pepper, diced

Quickly blanch carrots, zucchini, broccoli and cauliflower. Set aside. Cook chicken in water, vinegar, soy sauce, garlic, bay leaves, pepper and sugar until chicken is cooked through; about 15-20 minutes. Allow to cool. Remove chicken, dice and set aside. Remove bay leaves. Reduce cooking liquid by half. Arrange all vegetables on a platter. Starting from the bottom, place the watercress first, then tomatoes and finally red pepper. Spoon cubed chicken and pour on sauce. Serve immediately.

Chicken Adobo Primavera

ADOBO MUSHROOMS

Serves 2

2 10-ounce packages white button mushrooms, trimmed and sliced into 1/4 -inch thick pieces
1/4 cup olive oil
1/4 cup rice wine vinegar
3 tablespoons soy sauce
1 tablespoon garlic, minced
3 bay leaves, dried
2 teaspoons Dijon mustard
1 teaspoon tabasco sauce
1/2 teaspoon freshly ground black pepper
1/4 cup scallions, chopped, for garnish

Saute mushrooms 4 to 5 minutes in oil. Add remaining ingredients and cook 18 to 20 minutes until sauce reduces to a glaze. Remove bay leaves. Sprinkle with scallions and serve hot.

Serving suggestion: Spoon adobo on top of prosciutto.

CORNISH HEN ADOBO

Serves 2

One 1 1/2 pound cornish hen, split down the back and flattened
3/4 cup white vinegar
1/2 cup water
1/4 cup soy sauce
8 cloves garlic, minced
1 1/2 teaspoon ground black pepper
1/2 teaspoon sugar
3 bay leaves

Preheat oven to broil setting (about 500° F).

Place all ingredients in a large pot and bring to a boil, then continue to cook on low heat for 30 minutes. Remove hen and broil in oven, skin side up in a roasting pan for 5 minutes or until golden brown and cooked through. Keep hen warm. In a small sauce pan, pour juices from the broiled hen. Boil until sauce is reduced to half; check seasoning. Arrange cornish hen on serving plate and pour sauce over and serve immediately.

Adobo Mushrooms

Prawns Adobo

PRAWNS ADOBO

Serves 4

1 pound fresh prawns or jumbo shrimp
1 1/2 tablespoons soy sauce
2 tablespoons vinegar
1 1/2 teaspoons garlic, chopped
2 tablespoons olive oil
1/2 cup water
1 bay leaf, dried
1/2 teaspoon black peppercorns

Peel fresh prawns or shrimp, devein and wash thoroughly. Place in a bowl. Add all other ingredients, cover and marinate in refrigerator for 1 hour. In a non-stick skillet, over medium-high heat, cook for 5 minutes or until done. Serve with steamed rice and pickled vegetables.

ADOBO WITH LIVER SAUCE

Serves 4

2 teaspoons annato seeds
1/4 cup olive oil
6 cloves garlic, crushed
1/2 pound stewing beef, cut into 1-inch cubes
1/2 pound stewing pork, cut into 1-inch cubes
1/2 cup red wine vinegar
2 tablespoons butter
1/2 pound chicken liver, trimmed

In a cup of boiling water, soak annato seeds 30 minutes. Crush seeds with fingers. Set aside liquid and discard seeds. In a small amount of oil, brown garlic and cubed meat. Add annato liquid and vinegar. Simmer covered, until meat is tender. Cover and keep warm. In a small skillet, melt butter and saute liver until cooked through. Transfer liver with a slotted spoon to a food processor and puree coarsely. Add to stew and cook uncovered. Reduce sauce until thick. Season to taste.

SAUTEED ADOBO SOFT SHELL CRABS ON HERBED TOAST

Serves 4

8 soft shell crabs
1 1-ounce package adobo sauce mix
4 tablespoons butter, divided
2 tablespoons vegetable oil
1/2 lemon
parsley, for garnish

Toasts:

4 tablespoons butter
4 slices white bread, cut in half, crusts removed
2 cloves garlic, minced
1/4 teaspoon dill leaves, dried

Pat crabs on both sides in the adobo mixture, shaking off excess. Heat 2 tablespoons butter with oil in a skillet and saute crabs, turning, once, about 4 minutes until golden. Add more oil if necessary. Arrange 2 toasts on each of 4 plates. In a small saucepan melt remaining 2 tablespoons butter. Squeeze in lemon. Pour over crabs. Garnish with parsley.

To prepare toasts, heat butter in skillet; saute bread with garlic turning until golden on each side. Sprinkle with dill and seve with crabs.

Chef's note: The adobo sauce mix is available in Asian specialty stores and in the Asian section of supermarkets.

EGGPLANT ADOBO

Serves 2

5 cups diced eggplant, cut in 1 1/2-inch cubes
salt to taste
1/4 to 1/2 cup vegetable oil
1/3 cup soy sauce
1/4 cup red wine vinegar
6 cloves garlic, minced
1/2 teaspoon freshly ground black pepper

Spread eggplant on paper toweling and sprinkle with salt. Let drain for 30 minutes. Rinse and pat dry. In a non-stick skillet, fry eggplant in oil until brown and set aside. In a small saucepan, simmer soy sauce, vinegar, garlic and pepper for 5 minutes. Add eggplant, cover and cook over low heat for 7 minutes, stirring occasionally. Serve hot.

CHICKEN ADOBO IN COCONUT MILK

Serves 2 to 4

2 tablespoons garlic, minced
1 onion, chopped
2 tablespoons olive oil
1 whole chicken, cut into 8-10 pieces
3 cups coconut milk, divided
1 teaspoon ground black pepper
1/4 teaspoon salt
1/4 teaspoon fresh ginger, grated
3 tablespoons vinegar
1 small piece chili (optional)

In a soup pot, saute garlic and onion in 2 tablespoons olive oil. Add chicken pieces, 2 cups coconut milk, black pepper, salt, ginger and vinegar. Bring to a boil and simmer uncovered until chicken is very tender, about 1 hour and 10 minutes. Add chili (optional to taste) to make dish hot and spicy. Add remaining coconut milk, stir and simmer 2 to 3 minutes until sauce is thick and oily. Serve hot over rice.

Chef's note: Coconut milk is found in Hispanic or Asian food sections in canned or powdered forms. If using powdered form, follow package instructions to make coconut milk.

GRILLED ADOBO PORK CHOPS

4 pork chops, 8 ounces each
8 cloves garlic, minced
3 cups white wine vinegar
3/4 cup sugar
3/4 cup soy sauce
1 tablespoon tabasco sauce
1 teaspoon salt
4 bay leaves, dried

Serves 4

Preheat oven to broil setting (about 500° F).

Place chops in a large bowl. Stir all remaining ingredients and pour over chops. Marinate up to 1 hour. Drain chops and grill or broil 12 minutes, basting every 3 minutes, until chops are cooked through. Serve at once.

BEANSPROUTS ADOBO

2 tablespoons corn oil
1 teaspoon sesame oil
1/2 pound ground pork
8 cloves garlic, minced
1/3 cup onion, chopped
1/2 pound large shrimp, peeled and deveined
5 cups beansprouts
3/4 cup water
1 1/2 tablespoons soy sauce
1 1/2 tablespoons vinegar
1/4 teaspoon pepper

Serves 4

In a large skillet, over medium heat, heat corn and sesame oil. Saute pork, garlic and onions until pork is no longer pink. Add shrimp and saute until pink, about 2 minutes. Stir in the beansprouts until well mixed; stir in remaining ingredients. Increase heat to high, cover and cook for 3 minutes. Serve immediately.

BARBECUE

Although the art of barbecuing and grilling was introduced with the arrival of the Americans, the Filipinos, used to outdoor living had most probably practiced this natural method of cooking long before.

Grilling, which many people loosely refer to as barbecuing, is fast cooking over extreme, dry heat, (500° F and above) on an open cooker. True barbecuing is slow, thorough cooking in hardwood smoke in an enclosed pit.

In the Philippines, barbecued meat is usually sprinkled with salt and pepper, or soy sauce and lemon juice. It is eaten with a sauce comprised of crushed garlic and vinegar. Other barbecue sauces are made from a combination of soy sauce, ketchup, brown sugar and lemon juice. The sauce is used to marinate raw meat for added flavor, to baste meat while it is cooking, and to serve with cooked meat as a condiment.

Barbecue is not limited to meat. Today, in the streets of Manila, one may stumble upon stalls selling barbecued bananas, sweet potatoes, corn, chicken feet, chicken entrails, and even pig's ears.

< Grilled Fish with Pineapple Salsa

BARBECUE SAUCE

1 cup banana catsup (One 8 ounce bottle)
1 cup light brown sugar, packed
1 cup soy sauce
1/4 cup lemon juice

Yields: 2 1/2 cups

Combine catsup, sugar, soy sauce and lemon juice in a small bowl. Use sauce as a marinade for pork, beef, lamb or chicken preferably overnight.

BARBECUED PORK SPARERIBS

5 pounds pork spareribs
salt and pepper to taste
1/2 cup catsup
1/4 cup lemon juice
2 tablespoons brown sugar
1 tablespoon Worcestershire sauce
1 tablespoon hot sauce

Serves 5

Preheat oven at 450° F.

Season spareribs with salt and pepper. Mix the catsup, lemon juice, brown sugar, Worstershire sauce and hot sauce in a small bowl. Coat both sides of the ribs. Cover and refrigerate for about one hour. Set spareribs curved side down on a rack over a roasting pan, turning every 30 minutes until fork tender, about 2 hours. Serve with pickled vegetables and baked potato or rice if desired.

Chef's note: It is best to marinate spareribs overnight. Remember to keep basting both sides with the remaining sauce while cooking. Make more sauce if needed. The slower cooking prescribed here removes more fat from the ribs. Ribs can be finished on the barbecue over hot, grey coals in the last 20 minutes of cooking or under the broiler on moderate heat.

Barbecued Pork Spareribs

1/3 cup ginger juice

1/3 cup lemon juice

1/4 cup lemon grass, chopped

1 teaspoon salt

1 1/2 teaspoons pepper

1 whole chicken (approximately 2 1/2–3 pounds)

CHICKEN BARBECUE
(*Inasal na Manok*)

Serves 4 to 6

Preheat oven to 450° F.

In a large bowl, stir together ginger juice, lemon juice, lemon grass, salt and pepper. Place chicken in bowl and turn to coat in marinade. Cover and refrigerate for 1 hour, turning chicken occasionally.

Roast chicken for 10 minutes; reduce heat to 350° F and continue to roast, basting frequently, until juices run clear when thigh joint is pierced with tip of sharp knife, about 1 hour. Remove chicken from oven and let stand for 10 minutes before cutting. Serve chicken with baked beans, pickled vegetables and peanut sauce.

Chef's note: To make ginger juice, peel and cut ginger into chunks and place in food processor. Blend peeled chunks to yield one 2/3 cup grated ginger; pass through food mill to extract 1/3 cup juice. Peanut sauce, may be found prepared in canned or bottled forms in Asian specialty stores or food sections of supermarkets. Garnish chicken with peanuts if desired.

- 1/2 cup soy sauce
- 1 small bunch lemon grass, chopped (white portion only)
- 6 garlic cloves, minced
- 1 tablespoon sesame seeds, toasted
- 1 teaspoon black pepper
- 1 teaspoon red pepper flakes
- 2 pounds pork ribs

PORK BARBECUE RIBS WITH LEMON GRASS

Serves 4

Preheat oven to broil setting or light charcoal.

In a large, non-corrosive bowl, mix soy sauce, lemon grass, garlic, sesame seeds, black pepper and pepper flakes. Add pork ribs and toss to coat in sauce. Cover and refrigerate overnight, tossing ribs in sauce occasionally. To cook ribs, remove from sauce and grill or broil, brushing with remaining barbecue sauce. Broil ribs, 6 inches from heat source, turning pieces to brown evenly, about 8-9 minutes. Reduce heat to 350° F and bake 20-25 minutes, brushing with barbecue sauce, until meat is fork tender.

Chef's note: If you do not have access to a grill, broiling in an oven yeilds the same results.

- 1/3 cup light molasses
- 2 tablespoons lime juice
- 1 teaspoon peppercorns, crushed
- 2 tablespoons + 2 teaspoons dark soy sauce
- 1 tablespoon sugar
- 1 chicken (about 3 1/2 pounds), cut into 10 pieces

CHICKEN BARBECUE (PRE-WAR RECIPE)

Serves 4

Preheat oven to broil setting or 500° F.

In a large bowl, mix molasses, lime juice, peppercorns, soy sauce and sugar; add chicken pieces and toss to coat with sauce. Cover and chill for 30 minutes. Bring

Pork Barbecue Ribs with Lemon Grass

chicken to room temperature 20 minutes before cooking. (Chicken may marinate up to 24 hours in sauce with occasional turning). Transfer chicken to roasting pan, reserving sauce. Broil 6 inches from heat source or until golden brown. Reduce heat to 350° F. Baste chicken with remaining sauce and bake until juices run clear when meat is pierced with tip of small sharp knife (about 11 to 13 minutes for breasts and 16 to 18 minutes for thighs and legs).

GRILLED PRAWNS IN GREEN MANGO AND ANCHOVY SAUCE

Serves 4

- **1 pound prawns or jumbo shrimp, shelled, deveined and butterflied**
- **salt and white pepper to taste**
- **fresh lemon juice**
- **1 whole green mango, pared and fruit sliced from pod or 1 cup bottled green mango pieces**
- **2 tablespoons white wine**
- **1/2 teaspoon anchovy paste (*bagoong* or baby shrimp paste)**
- **1 medium shallot, chopped**
- **3 tablespoons unsalted butter**

Light charcoal or preheat oven to broil setting.

Season prawns or shrimps with salt and pepper to taste; drizzle lightly with lemon juice; set aside. In a medium-size saucepan, place mango and enough water to cover. Bring to a boil over high heat and reduce heat. Simmer until soft, about 5 minutes; drain. Place mango, wine and anchovy paste (*bagoong*) in a food processor; blend until smooth. In a small saucepan, saute shallots in butter over medium heat until softened, about 5 minutes. Stir in pureed mango mixture and cook briefly to heat

through. Season with salt and pepper to taste. (If sauce is too thick, thin with 1-2 tablespoons hot water). Grill prawns or shrimps over charcoal or broil in oven. Pour sauce over prawns or serve on the side.

GRILLED FISH WITH PINEAPPLE SALSA

Serves 4

1/3 cup rice wine vinegar
1/2 cup onion, minced
2 teaspoons ginger, minced and divided
salt and pepper to taste
1 teaspoon Dijon mustard
4 fish fillets (6 ounces each, sole or halibut)
1/2 medium-sized pineapple, peeled, cored and diced (1 1/2 cups)
1 small red pepper, diced (1/2 cup)
1 long chili pepper, minced
1 tablespoon lemon juice

In a large non-corrosive shallow baking dish or container, stir together vinegar, onion, 1 teaspoon ginger and mustard. Add fish fillets and toss to coat; cover and refrigerate 30 minutes. In a medium bowl, mix pineapple, red pepper, chili, lemon juice, remaining ginger, salt and pepper to make salsa. Cover and refrigerate. Broil fillets, 6 inches from heat source until fish is cooked. Serve with salsa.

DESSERTS

Philippine cuisine prides itself on its variety of desserts. The dessert menu is rich with native cakes made from different kinds of rice cooked with coconut milk and eaten with fresh or preserved fruits. Filipinos have mastered the baking of American cakes and pies, substituting native fruits and vegetables. The wide assortment of native fruits provides an endless source from which to make jams and preserves, sherbets, ice cream and cakes. The Philippine fruit salad, originally made of canned fruits and fresh coconut strands mixed with condensed milk and Nestle's cream, is a divine concoction. There is also *Sans Rival*, a delicious layered cake of Spanish origin, made of mixed egg whites, sugar and chopped cashew nuts.

< *Tropical Cream with Papaya Coulis*

BANANA MOUSSE WITH CHOCOLATE GINGER SAUCE

1 teaspoon gelatin powder
1/4 cup lukewarm water
4 ripe bananas, peeled and cut into pieces
1 cup powdered sugar, divided
4 large egg whites, at room temperature
1/8 teaspoon cream of tartar
2 cups heavy cream
1/4 teaspoon vanilla extract

Sauce:
1 cup cocoa powder
3/4 cup water
3/4 cup sugar
1 cup cream
2 tablespoons grated ginger
1 teaspoon Kahlua (or any coffee liqueur)

Serves 8 to 10

In a glass measuring cup, soften powdered gelatin by sprinkling gelatin over the water; heat slowly until dissolved. In a blender or food processor, puree bananas with 1/2 cup powdered sugar. Add dissolved gelatin and blend briefly to incorporate; set aside. In a large mixing bowl, beat egg whites on low setting of electric mixer until foamy. Add cream of tartar and mix on high until thickened. While mixing, gradually add remaining powdered sugar and beat until soft peaks form; transfer into a bowl and set aside. In same mixing bowl, beat heavy cream on medium setting of electric mixer until thickened; increase speed to high, add vanilla and beat until soft peaks form. Add beaten egg whites to whipped cream and fold briefly together to incorporate. Add 1/4 of the white-cream mixture to banana mixture and stir until well mixed. Add banana mixture to remaining egg white-cream mixture and fold until incorporated. Cover and chill for 4 hours or until set.

To make sauce: heat cocoa and water together until dissolved in a medium-size saucepan. Over low heat, stir mixture until hot and thickened. Add sugar, cream and

ginger; increase heat to medium and bring mixture to boil, stirring constantly, about 5 minutes. Mixture should be thick enough to coat a spoon; if not, continue to boil while stirring constantly for another 2-3 minutes until thickened. Strain sauce into a sauce boat or small bowl and stir in the Kahlua. Serve sauce warm or cool.

Chef's note: Mousse yields approximately 8 cups volume and sauce yields 2 1/2 cups.

COUPE GIANNINA

Serves 2 to 4

1 1/2 cups sugar
1/4 cup water
1/2 cup (1 stick) unsalted butter, cut into 5 pieces
2 bananas, cut into 1/4-inch slices
1 medium ripe mango, pared, seed removed and flesh cut into 1/2-inch pieces (1 1/2 cups)
2 teaspoons lemon peel, grated
1 teaspoon orange peel, grated
2 tablespoons Curacao liqueur

In a medium, heavy-bottomed saucepan, over medium-high heat, bring sugar and water to boil; cook uncovered, until syrup turns golden brown, about 15 minutes. (Do not stir syrup while it is cooking; saucepan may be gently swirled. Moisten inside of pan with pastry brush dipped in water to prevent sugar syrup from crystallizing.) Immediately remove saucepan from heat. Add butter, stirring with wooden spoon until incorporated; stir in banana, mango, lemon peel, orange peel and Curacao until well mixed. Set mixture aside to cool for 20 minutes, stirring occasionally. Chill until ready to serve.

Chef's note: This dish is delicious served over vanilla ice cream.

FRESH FRUIT CALYPSO

Serves 6

2 medium Navel oranges, peeled and cut into 1-inch pieces
2 medium bananas, peeled and sliced into 1/2-inch pieces
1/2 ripe medium papaya, pared, seeded and cut into 1-inch cubes
1 large peach, peeled and cut into 1-inch cubes
6 strawberries, sliced into quarters
1/2 cup lemon juice
1/3 cup sugar
vanilla ice cream or yogurt
whipped cream

In a medium-size glass bowl, combine fruits; sprinkle with lemon juice and sugar; toss briefly to coat fruit with lemon and sugar. Cover and chill fruit mixture for at least 1 hour. To serve, scoop desired amount of ice cream or yogurt into large serving bowl. Spoon over fruit mixture and top with whipped cream.

Chef's note: Other fresh fruits in season may be substituted as desired. Maple syrup may be used instead of sugar.

STEAMED YUCCA PATTIES WITH GRATED COCONUT

Serves 6 to 8 (Yields 24 to 32 pieces)

3 cups grated cassava (yucca)
1 cup granulated sugar (use dark brown sugar if more color is preferred)
1/2 teaspoon baking soda
1 cup unsweetened coconut, grated

Squeeze grated cassava to remove starch; put into a mixing bowl. Add sugar and baking soda and mix thoroughly until smooth. Roll one tablespoon of mix, press between palms of hands and place pressed mix (pattie) inside a greased muffin pan (1 1/2-inch diameter mini muffin). Boil water in steamer and steam pans for 20 minutes, covered, on top of stove. Remove from pan and roll in grated coconut and serve warm or in room temperature.

MANGO BAVARIAN WITH WHITE CHOCOLATE SAUCE

Serves 8

4 large egg yolks
10 ounces white chocolate, finely chopped
1/2 cup heavy cream
2 tablespoons white creme de cacao or 1 tablespoon chocolate extract
4 medium mangoes, pared, pod removed and flesh chopped (about 4 cups)
6 tablespoons sugar
6 tablespoons water
2 packets gelatin (4 teaspoons)
2 cups heavy cream, divided
1/2 cup chocolate syrup

To make white chocolate sauce, place egg yolks in a medium-size bowl. Place white chocolate in another medium glass bowl. In a large bowl, place 12-14 ice cubes; set all aside. In a medium-size, heavy-bottomed saucepan, over high heat, bring cream to a boil, stirring constantly. In the bowl with egg yolks, gradually whisk in the hot cream. Return mixture of egg yolks and cream to saucepan and cook over low heat, stirring constantly, until mixture coats the back of a wooden spoon. Pour hot yolk mixture over white chocolate, stirring until chocolate is melted and incorporated; stir in white creme de cacao. Place bowl with the mixture in the iced bowl and continue stirring until sauce is cool to touch; cover and chill.

For Mango Bavarian: In a large saucepan, add mango, sugar and water. Bring mixture to boil over medium heat; lower heat and simmer 5 minutes until thickened. Transfer mixture to a blender or food processor; blend 1 minute until smooth. Meanwhile, place 1/4 cup of the cream in a glass measuring cup; sprinkle gelatin over cream. In microwave oven, cook cream mixture on high 20-30 seconds until cream begins to boil; stir to dissolve gelatin. Stir cream mixture into mango puree; set aside. In a large-size chilled bowl, with electric mixer on medium, whip remaining cream until thickened; increase speed to high and whip until soft peaks are formed. Add 1/4 of the whipped cream to the mango puree; stir until well combined. Return mango mixture to bowl with whipped cream; fold mixtures together until combined. Spoon mango bavarian into mold or individual serving bowls, cover and chill 4 hours until set. To serve, place white chocolate sauce on the base of individual serving plates; unmold mango bavarian on middle of each plate. Drizzle chocolate syrup along border of the plate; using a sharp knife make a decorative design by cutting dark chocolate sauce into light chocolate sauce.

ATIS (*Cherimoya*) MOUSSE WITH CHICO WHISKEY SAUCE

Serves 12

25 ounces *atis* fruit, coarsely chopped
5 tablespoons powdered sugar
1/2 teaspoon vanilla extract
2 packets gelatin mixture (approximately 4 teaspoons) dissolved in 6 tablespoons warm water and simmered until warm and clear
4 large egg whites
2-4 drops lemon juice
1 cup heavy cream, whipped
Chico (*sapodilla*) Whiskey Sauce (recipe follows)

Sauce:

1 pound chico (*sapodilla*) fruit, peeled and seeded
1 teaspoon heavy cream
2 tablespoons sugar
2 tablespoons whiskey or bourbon
1 teaspoon cinnamon

Cut atis (*cherimoya*) fruit in half and scrape out all pulp. Remove seeds by pressing fruit through a course strainer; discard seeds. In a food processor or blender, combine pulp, powdered sugar, vanilla extract and dissolved gelatin mixture. Blend until smooth; set aside. In a large bowl, with an electric mixer on medium, beat the egg whites until foamy. Sprinkle the lemon juice into the whites and beat until soft peaks form. Fold in the whipped cream and fruit mixture. Store in freezer until ready to use.

To make sauce, combine chico (sapodilla) fruit, heavy cream, sugar, whiskey and cinnamon in food processor or blender. Blend until smooth. Pour over mousse mixture and garnish with a sprinkle of cinnamon

TROPICAL CREAM WITH PAPAYA COULIS

Serves 6

1 envelope unflavored gelatin
1 cup + 1/4 cup heavy cream, divided
1/4 cup canned coconut cream
1/4 cup sugar
1 cup strawberries
1 medium banana peeled and cut into pieces (1/2 cup)
1 1/2 tablespoons lime juice
3/4 cup goats milk or yogurt
2 tablespoons light rum
6 strawberries, for garnish

Coulis:

1/4 cup sugar
1/4 cup water
1 medium papaya (10 ounces), peeled, seeded and cut into chunks
1 tablespoon lime juice

In a small saucepan, sprinkle gelatin over 1/4 cup of the heavy cream; let stand l minute. Stir in coconut cream and sugar. Over medium heat, stir mixture until gelatin is dissolved; remove from heat and cool briefly. Whip l cup heavy cream in a chilled medium bowl until soft peaks form; chill. In a food processor or blender, purée strawberries, banana, lime juice and yogurt. While machine is running, pour in gelatin mixture and rum. Fold fruit mixture into whipped cream and pour into six individual glasses. Cover and chill until set, about 3 hours. Meanwhile, prepare papaya coulis by combining sugar and water in a small sauce pan. Bring to a boil stirring until sugar is completely dissolved. Remove from heat and cool. In a food processor, combine papaya, sugar-syrup and lime juice; blend until smooth. Cover and refrigerate. To serve, pour papaya coulis on top of the individual tropical cream desserts. Garnish with strawberries.

Sweet Bananas with Sesame Seed Butter Sauce

SWEET BANANAS WITH SESAME SEED BUTTER SAUCE

Serves 4 to 6

- 3 medium plantains
- 2 tablespoons unsalted butter
- 1/4 cup light brown sugar, firmly packed
- 1/4 cup sesame seeds, toasted
- 4 teaspoons lemon juice
- vanilla ice cream (1-2 scoops per person)

Peel plantains and cut lengthwise into halves. Cut halves crosswise into 2 pieces. In a large non-stick skillet, over medium heat, cook butter until foaming subsides. Add the banana pieces and saute until golden brown, about 2 minutes per side. Reserving butter in skillet, remove bananas to a dish and keep warm. In same skillet, over medium-low heat, stir brown sugar into remaining butter until dissolved; stir in sesame seeds and lemon juice. Pour sauce over bananas. Serve as is or best topped with vanilla ice cream.

LIGHT AND FRUITY CARAMEL CUSTARD

Serves 6

- 1 1/3 cup sugar, divided
- 1/3 cup water
- 6 to 8 large eggs
- 1 cup whole milk
- 1 cup peach or mango puree
- pinch of salt
- 1/4 teaspoon lime peel, grated finely
- seasonal fresh berries, for garnish

Preheat oven to 350° F.

Make a caramel using 1 cup sugar and 1/3 cup water. Pour into a 5 cup gratin or souffle dish. In a bowl, whisk eggs, milk, remaining 1/3 cup sugar, puree and salt.

Add grated lime peel, stir and pour into prepared pan. Place in a *bain-marie.* Bake in oven until a toothpick inserted halfway between center and edge comes out clean, about 50 minutes to 1 hour. Let cool to room temperature. Chill at least 1 to 2 hours. Unmold onto serving platter and garnish with seasonal fresh berries as desired.

Chef's note: Gratin or souffle dish may be aluminum or ceramic. Bain-marie is the term used for cooking through steam in a water bath. The dish is placed in a larger pan half-filled with water and placed into a preheated oven or a steamer.

FRESH FRUIT AND SHAVED ICE WITH COCONUT MILK (*Halo-Halo Ilustrado*)

Serves 4

2 cups fresh cubed fruit, such as kiwi, melon, whole grapes or any sweet fruit of your choice
1/2 cup water
1/4 cup light brown sugar
2 tablespoons fresh lemon grass, sliced (white part only)
1 cup coconut milk (unsweetened)
10 ice cubes
sliced almonds, for garnish

Spoon cubed fruit into 4 large glasses. Set aside. In a small saucepan over high heat, combine water, sugar and lemon grass. Cook until sugar is dissolved; set aside to cool. Pour cooled syrup into glasses with fruit. In a blender, whirl coconut milk with 10 ice cubes, dropping in cubes 1 at a time, until thick and frothy. Spoon onto fruit. Garnish with sliced almonds.

Chef's note: Coconut milk is found canned or powdered in Asian specialty stores.

PINEAPPLE AND COCONUT SORBET WITH TUILES

- **1 cup coconut juice, unsweetened**
- **1 cup coconut cream**
- **3/4 cup confectioners sugar (optional)**
- **4 cups pineapple juice, strained through fine sieve**
- **24 pieces thin round butter cookies**

Serves 8

In a large bowl, mix coconut juice, coconut cream and sugar until well combined. Stir in pineapple juice. Pour into two 9-inch cake pans and freeze until set, about 4 hours. Stir each mixture occasionally to enhance even freezing. Scoop sorbet into individual serving bowls and serve with 2 or 3 butter cookies.

Chef's note: Tuiles or thin butter wafers are available at specialty gourmet food shops or European patisseries. If using canned pineapple juice, pick the unsweetened variety.

PLANTAIN (*Saba*) SOUFFLE WITH CHOCOLATE CINNAMON SAUCE

Serves 10

2 cups ripe sweet plantains, removed from skin
1/4 cup heavy cream
5 tablespoons sugar
2 yolks
2 to 3 drops banana extract
5 egg whites
1/4 teaspoon cream of tartar
10 large semi-ripe plantain skin halves, carved into boats

Sauce:

1/2 cup half and half
2 tablespoons chocolate syrup
2 tablespoons brandy or Kahlua (coffee liqueur)
1/2 teaspoon cinnamon
1 tablespoon unsalted butter

Preheat oven to 350° F.

In a food processor or blender, blend plantains, cream, sugar, yolks and extract until smooth, about 1 minute, chill. In a mixer bowl, beat whites until foamy; add cream of tartar and beat until thick but not dry. Stir 1/4 of beaten egg whites into chilled plantain mixture; fold puree mixture into remaining whites. Spoon mixture into skins. Bake 13-15 minutes until puffy and light. Meanwhile, in a small saucepan, stirring constantly, bring to boil 1/2 cup half and half, 2 tablespoons chocolate syrup, 2 tablespoons brandy or Kahlua and 1/2 teaspoon cinnamon. Remove saucepan from heat and add 1 tablespoon butter and stir until shiny. Pour over plaintain souffle or serve on the side.

Chef's note: It may also be good to prebake or warm plantain skins before spooning in souffle mixture.

CHEFS AND THEIR RECIPES

•

SUGGESTED MENUS

•

ACKNOWLEDGMENTS

REGGIE AGUINALDO

1. Sweet Corn Soup with Herbs p. 52
2. Pan de Sal Garlic Toasties p. 26
3. Native Lettuce Greens with Milkfish Salad p. 71
4. Fresh Fruit Calypso p. 157
5. Deluxe Mongo Soup p. 54
6. Fish Slices in Rice Wine Sauce p. 81
7. Steamed Garlic Rice p. 38
8. Ensalada Filipina with Thick Garlic Dressing p. 67
9. Sweet Bananas with Sesame Butter Sauce p. 170
10. Shrimp and Cucumber Soup p. 52
11. Light and Fruity Caramel Custard p. 170
12. Pasta with Pimiento and Bacon Sauce p. 40

REYNALDO ALEJANDRO

1. Adobo Mushrooms p. 132
2. Eggplant Adobo p. 137
3. Adobo Soft Shell Crabs on Herbed Toast p. 136
4. Prawns Adobo p. 135
5. Chicken Adobo Primavera p. 129
6. Adobo with Liver Sauce p. 135
7. Hamburger Adobo p. 129
8. Grilled Adobo Porkchops p. 138
9. Cornish Hen Adobo p. 132

HENRY CANOY

1. Fresh Fruit and Shaved Ice with Coconut Milk p. 171
2. Herbal Fumet with Tapioca p. 49
3. Fish Bisque with Puff Pastry p. 84
4. Consomme of Lamb p. 46
5. Smoked Chicken with Goat Cheese p. 123
6. Beer Braised lamb Stew. p. 94
7. Grilled Fish with Pineapple Salsa p. 150
8. Pork and Vegetables Stewed in Tomato and Anchovy Paste p. 115
9. Grilled Prawns in Green Mango and Anchovy Sauce p. 148
10. Pollo Carolina p. 122
11. Zarzuela Salad p. 58

SANDY DAZA

GENE GONZALEZ

BAMBINA HERBOSA (ROSEMARIE)

4. Pork Barbecue Ribs with Lemon Grass p. 146

5. Winged Beans with Shrimp p. 89

6. Sesame Cheese Sticks p. 33

7. Native Mushroom Soup with Pepper Leaves p. 51

8. Watercress, Beansprout and Avocado Salad p. 59

9. Fiddlehead Ferns with Ginger and Coconut p. 70

10. Seafood Stew with Coriander p. 83

CELY KALAW

1. Pickled Anchovies p. 26

2. Fried Baby Shrimp Fritters p. 37

3. Shrimp Bisque p. 51

4. Chicken Adobo in Coconut Milk p. 137

5. Rolled Carp Poached in Coconut Milk p. 38

6. Bitter Melon Salad p. 59

7. Mustard Leaves Salad p. 67

8. Steamed Yucca Patties with Grated Coconut (Pichi-Pichi) p. 157

9. Chilled Coconut Cream and Corn Gelatin p. 160

10. Banana Leaf Wrapped and Stewed Prawns p. 78

11. Baked Stuffed Pompano p. 80

DULCE MAGAT

1. Baked Mussels with Pesto and Mozzarella Cheese p. 28

2. Smoked Mackerel Bisque p. 47

3. Round Scrod Fillet with Warm Herbed Vinaigrette p. 76

4. Steamed Grouper (Lapu-Lapu) with Vegetable Julienne p. 90

5. Grilled Duck with Mango Anise Sauce p. 108

6. Pineapple and Coconut Sorbet with Tuiles p. 172

7. Pili Nut Souffle p. 162

8. Tropical Cream with Papaya Coulis p. 167

MILLIE REYES

1. Seafood Cocktail p. 34

2. Shrimp in Coconut Milk p. 86

3. Crab Cakes p. 35
4. Chicken Steak with Beansprouts p. 103
5. Whole Stuffed Chicken Relleno p. 124
6. Chicken Barbecue (Inasal na Manok) p. 145
7. Beef Mechado p. 121
8. Barbecued Pork Spareribs p. 142

NANCY REYES

1. Filipino Springrolls p. 24
2. Chicken with Beer p. 112
3. Chicken Pasolo p. 98
4. Lobster Aux Fruits p. 62
5. Chicken Barbecue (Prewar Recipe) p. 146
6. Bell Peppers Nancy p. 33

The following are suggested menus derived from the recipes featured in the book. They range from the simple to the more elaborate depending on the occasion and one's preferences. The simple menu plans contain either a soup or a salad, a main dish and a dessert. They range from combinations of soup and salads to more substantial repasts of salad and fish or meat courses with rice. The elegant and more festive menu plans are more elaborate and contain an appetizer, a salad, a choice from two entrees and two desserts. The buffet menu plans list several dishes that can be served together for more festive occasions. There are a couple of menu plans for vegetarians but there are many more recipes that may be made vegetarian by simply substituting the seafood or meats with wheat gluten or tofu. The brunch menu plans feature lighter combinations of appetizers, salads, main courses and desserts. In time, as you sample and get more acquainted with the recipes, you will be able to devise your own menus from the variety provided in this book.

SIMPLE MENU PLANS

Menu 1:

Sweet Corn Soup with Herbs
Steamed Grouper (*Lapu-Lapu*) w/ Vegetables Julienne
or
Beef Tenderloin in Papaya Seed Sauce
Mustard Leaves Salad

Pineapple and Coconut Sorbet

Menu 2:

Sesame Cheese Sticks with Consomme of Lamb
Native Lettuce Greens with Milkfish Salad
or
Roast Chicken with Passion Fruit Sauce
Fiddlehead Ferns with Ginger and Coconut

Fresh Fruit Calypso

Menu 3:

Steamed Garlic Rice
Chicken Steak with Beansprouts
or
Pickled Vegetables with Quail Eggs
Pork Barbecue Ribs with Lemon Grass

Sweet Bananas with Sesame Seed Butter Sauce

ELEGANT AND FESTIVE MENU PLANS

Menu 1:

Crab Cakes
Zarzuela Salad

Pollo Carolina
or
Roasted Lamb with Dayap Leaves

Chirimoya Mousse with Chico Whiskey Sauce
or
Banana Mousse with Chocolate Ginger Sauce

Menu 2:

Bell Peppers Nancy
Stuffed Yellow Squash Blossom Soup
Ensalada Filipina with Thick Garlic Dressing

Grilled Duck with Mango Anise Sauce
or
Grilled Prawns in Green Mango and Anchovy Sauce

Pili Nut Souffle
or
Plaintain Souffle with Chocolate Cinnamon Sauce

Menu 3:

Ube Soup with Pancit Molo
Watercress, Beansprout and Avocado Salad with Cilantro Sesame Dressing

Whole Stuffed Chicken Relleno
or
Beef Mechado

Coupe Giannina
or
Saba Souffle with White Chocolate Suace

VEGETARIAN MENU PLANS

Menu 1:

Herbal Fumet with Tapioca
Bitter Melon Salad
Pineapple and Coconut Sorbet with Tuiles

Menu 2:

Native Mushroom Soup
Beansprouts Adobo (with Tofu)*
Steamed Garlic Rice
Fresh Fruit and Shaved Ice with Coconut Milk (Halo Halo)

BUFFET MENU PLANS

Menu 1:

Baked Mussels with Pesto and Mozzarella Cheese
Pinoy Spring Rolls
Deluxe Mongo Soup
Ensalada Filipina with Thick Garlic Dressing
Winged Beans with Shrimp
Pastel of Chicken
Pork Roll
Chilled Corn and Coconut Cream Gelatin (Majadera)
Light Fruity Caramel Custard

Menu 2:

Fried Baby Shrimp Fritters (Tagonton Ukoy)
Meatballs with Sticky Rice
Shrimp and Cucumber Soup
Fiddlehead Ferns with Ginger and Coconut
Pickled Vegetables with Quail Eggs
Steamed Garlic Rice
Chicken Adobo in Coconut Milk
Angel Quails in Gin and Raisin Sauce
Pork Barbecue Ribs with Lemon Grass
Lamb in Mustard Crust wth Banana Blossom Sauce
Steamed Yucca Patties with Grated Coconut
Tropical Cream with Papaya Coulis

BRUNCH MENU PLANS

Menu 1:

Pan de Sal Garlic Toasties

Zarzuela Salad

Lobster Aux Fruits

or

Smoked Chicken with Goat Cheese

Pili Nut Souffle

Menu 2:

Seafood Cocktail

Grilled Fish with Pineapple Salsa

or

Debbie's Chicken Salad

Coupe Giannina

Menu 3:

Chicken Adobo Primavera

Fresh Fruit Calypso

or

Crispy Mung-Bean Noodles with Crab

Atis Mousse with Chico Whiskey Sauce

First and foremost, I would like to thank the outstanding chefs who made this book possible. Special thanks to Reynaldo Alejandro for his early encouragement and to Reggie Aguinaldo for her help in testing the recipes and looking after various administrative details.

I am also grateful to Penny Sibal Samonte for pointing me in the right direction and to Kevin Clark, my editor, for his untiring efforts to get this book done. Thanks to my creative team- Bill McConnell for the beautiful photography, Roscoe Betsill for the inspired food styling and Chris Thompson, for the imaginative book design. My enduring thanks to Sidney Burstein who did the initial testing of the recipes and whose untimely passing has left a void in the world of food styling.

I would also like to thank Patis Tesoro for the unusual and beautiful fabric fragments used throughout this book and Chris Thompson for the other wonderful props and objects.

My appreciation also goes to Bonjin Bolinao for her unflagging devotion to all my projects, to Bobby de la Fuente for all the legal advice, and to Louie Reyes for being a guide and mentor. Heartfelt thanks to the Philippine Department of Tourism, Philippine Air Lines, the Manila Hotel and the Mandarin Oriental Manila Hotel for their generosity and support for this project.

Lastly, my deepest gratitude to my husband Bill, for his love and encouragement, to my children, Alvi, Ria, Acacia and William for being an endless source of inspiration, and to our beloved nanny, Lilian Rada, for sharing her expertise on Philippine food.

INDEX

A

B

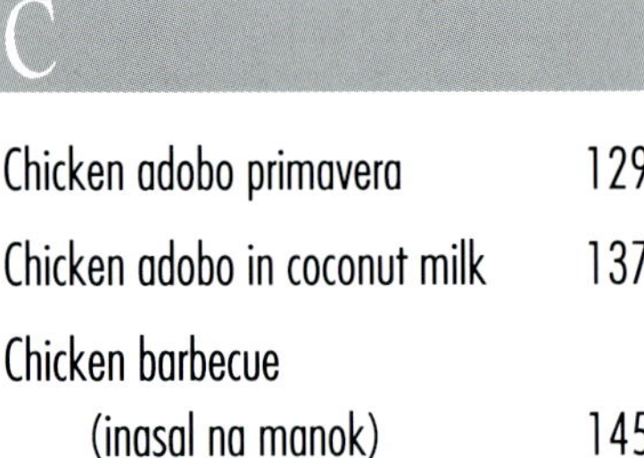

C

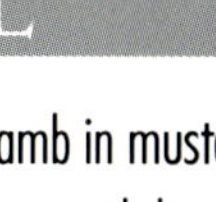

Simex
SALTED
TINY SHRIMPS
(PATE DE CREVETTE)
BAGOONG ALAMANG
KEEP REFRIGERATED
SIMEX INTERNATIONAL
NET WT. 12 OZ.
(340 g)

M

N

P

R

S

T

W

Z

The following list contains names, addresses and telephone numbers of retailers specializing in Asian food stuffs. Other retailers such as gourmet food markets and large supermarket chains may also carry some of the ingredients mentioned in PACIFIC CROSSINGS, as well as some specialty food stores and catalogers.

California

99 Ranch Market
1688 Hostetter Road
San Jose, CA
(408) 436-8899

Alegria Oriental Store
1601 Marine World Parkway, #135
Vallejo, CA
(707) 554-3835

Anna's Oriental Grocery
1306 W. Texas St.
Fairfield, CA
(707) 429-3106

Asian Import Mart
1511 Sycamore Ave., Ste. K
Hercules, CA
(510) 799-0379

Begal Import & Export
800 Cortland St.
San Francisco, CA
(415) 647-5208

Bulakena Grocery
4995 Mission St.
San Francisco, CA
(415) 334-3113

Asian Mini Market 4
3848 McKinley, Ste. 1A
Corona, CA 91719
(714) 278-2448

Golden Pacific Foods, Inc.
15451 Proctor Ave.
City of Industry, CA 91745
(818) 330-1641

Hop Fong Market, Inc.
1222-1224 W. Francisquito Ave.
W. Covina, CA 91790
(818) 917-3226

Bread Ranch
13373 Perris Blvd., Ste. 302-D
Moreno Valley, CA 92553
(714) 247-7771

JHL Trading Enterprises
3317 Burton Ave.
Burbank, CA 91504
(818) 558-1093

Crab-Co
8660 Miramar Rd., Ste. H
San Diego, CA
(619) 578-5870

Holgado Seafoods
13015 Abing Ave.
San Diego, CA
(619) 484-7048

Illinois

DCJ Oriental Food Mart
1109 North Western Ave.
Chicago, IL
(312) 235-2224

F&C Oriental Store
1300 C S, Main St.
Lombard, IL
(312) 620-5544

Oakton Oriental Food Store
4515 W. Oakton St.
Skokie, IL
(708) 673-3775

Silahis Oriental Food
648 Meacham Rd.
Elk Grove Village, IL

Connecticut

Fil-Asian Food
1127 Main St.
East Hartford, CT
(203) 291-8727

Hawaii

Amor Nino Foods, Inc.
766 Puuhale Rd., #101
Honolulu, HI
(808) 845-1711

Elena's Import
94-670 Farrington Highway
Waipahu, HI
(808) 671-4148

Hawaii Integrated, Inc.
815 Gullick Ave.
Honolulu, HI
(808) 847-1553

Lingayen Fish Market
719 Kam Highway
Pearl City, HI
(808) 455-5104

New Jersey

Alex's Filipino Store
326 North Ave., Box 213
Dunellen, NJ
(908) 968-9685

American-Pinoy Foodmart
1347 Kennedy Blvd.
Bayonne, NJ
(201) 436-7587

American-Pinoy Supermart
108 S. Front St.
Bergenfield, NJ
(201) 387-7979

Bayanihan
71 Franklin St.
Belleville, NJ
(201) 751-4332

Donna's Minimart
1259 Liberty Ave.
Hillside, NJ
(908) 289-8399

Filipino Family Foodmart
469 Main St.
Orange, NJ
(908) 752-4977

Fil-Orient Foodmart
427 West Side Ave.
Jersey City, NJ
(201) 435-6716

Maharlika Orient
128 Main Ave.
Passaic, NJ
(201) 778-7790

Oriental Delights
922 South Elmora Ave.
Elizabeth, NJ
(908) 351-9511

New York

Asian Best
1658 Middle Country Rd.
Centereach, NY
(516) 732-7336

Asia Food Market
71 1/2 Mulberry St.
New York, NY
(212) 962-2020

Bangkok-Manila Grocery
30-81 31st
Astoria, NY
(718) 565-9811

Chinese Manila Food
860 Tenth Ave.
New York, NY
(212) 489-5604

DMG Foodmart
3168 Coney Island Ave.
Brooklyn, NY
(718) 891-2022

Far East Enterprises
234 East Gun Hill Rd.
Bronx, NY
(212) 515-8405

Far East Mart
303 Rte. 59
West Nyack Mini Mall
West Nyack, NY
(914) 358-5551

Filipinas Enterprises
126 Lake Ave.
Yonkers, NY
(914) 476-0480

Garcia's Fil-Mart
3555 Victory Blvd.
Staten Island, NY
(718) 370-1746

Nayong Filipino
129 South Regent St.
Port Chester, NY
(914) 937-1741

Pearl Orient Foods
75 Atlantic Ave.
Brooklyn, NY
(718) 875-4435

Ohio

Bayanihan Food Inc.
625 Bolivar
Cleveland, OH 44101

Pennsylvania

Chinese and Oriental Food Product Research, Inc.
117 N. 10th St.
Philadelphia, PA 19107

Phil-Am Food Mart
5601 Camac
Philadelphia, PA 19104

Texas

Eastern Food Market
7801 Canal
Houston, TX 77012

First Oriental Market
904 St. Emanuel
Houston, TX 77042

Little Home Bakery
2109 Parker Rd., Ste. 202 A
Plano, TX 75023

Virginia

Manila Mart
3610 Lee Highway
Arlington, VA 22207

Washington

City Produce
701 7th Ave. South
Seattle, WA 98104

Fiesta Filipina Store
522 6th Ave. South
Seattle, WA 98104

Umajimaya, Inc.
519 6th Ave. South
Seattle, WA 98104

Canada

(Ontario)

Filipino Market
4 Irwin Ave.
Toronto, ON
Canada

Philippine Products
Sari-Sari Store
507-B Gladstone Ave.
Ottawa, ON
Canada

(Quebec)

Philippine Sari-Sari Store
4939 Cote des Neiges
Montreal, QE
Canada

DE STA